First World War
and Army of Occupation
War Diary
France, Belgium and Germany

36 DIVISION
Headquarters, Branches and Services
Royal Army Veterinary Corps
Assistant Director Veterinary Services
1 October 1915 - 24 March 1919

WO95/2495/3

The Naval & Military Press Ltd
www.nmarchive.com
Published in association with The National Archives

Published by

The Naval & Military Press Ltd

Unit 10 Ridgewood Industrial Park,

Uckfield, East Sussex,

TN22 5QE England

Tel: +44 (0) 1825 749494

www.naval-military-press.com

www.nmarchive.com

This diary has been reprinted in facsimile from the original. Any imperfections are inevitably reproduced and the quality may fall short of modern type and cartographic standards.

© **Crown Copyright**
Images reproduced by permission of The National Archives, London, England, 2015.

Contents

Document type	Place/Title	Date From	Date To
Miscellaneous	WO95/2495/3		
Heading	36th Division Divl Troops Asst Dir. Vety Services Oct 1915-Mar 1919		
Heading	36th Division H.Q. 36th Division A.D.V.S Vol I Oct 15		
War Diary	Bordon	01/10/1915	04/10/1915
War Diary	Flesselles	05/10/1915	22/10/1915
War Diary	Domart	23/10/1915	31/10/1915
Heading	H.Q. 36th Division A.D.V.S Vol 2 Nov 15		
War Diary	Domart	01/11/1915	29/11/1915
War Diary	Pont Remy	30/11/1915	30/11/1915
Heading	A.D.W. 36th Div. Vol. 3		
War Diary	Pontremy	01/12/1915	31/12/1915
Heading	A.D.M. 36th Div Vol 4 Jan 16		
War Diary	Pont Remy	01/01/1916	04/01/1916
War Diary	Domart	05/01/1916	18/01/1916
War Diary	Bernaville	19/01/1916	31/01/1916
Heading	A.D.M. 36th Div. Vol. 5		
War Diary	Bernaville	01/02/1916	06/02/1916
War Diary	Acheux	07/02/1916	29/02/1916
Heading	ADVS 36th Div Vol 6		
War Diary	Acheux	01/03/1916	02/04/1916
War Diary	Harponville	03/04/1916	20/04/1916
War Diary	Hedauville	21/04/1916	05/07/1916
War Diary	Rubempre	06/07/1916	09/07/1916
War Diary	Bernaville	10/07/1916	11/07/1916
War Diary	Blaringham	11/07/1916	12/07/1916
War Diary	Tilques	13/07/1916	20/07/1916
War Diary	Esquelbecq	02/07/1916	22/07/1916
War Diary	Mont Noir	23/07/1916	23/07/1916
War Diary	Bailleul	24/07/1916	14/10/1916
War Diary	Routine	15/10/1916	18/10/1916
War Diary	Bailleul	19/10/1916	06/04/1917
War Diary	St Jeans Capell	07/04/1917	14/05/1917
War Diary	Dranoutre	15/05/1917	20/05/1917
War Diary	Ulster Camp Dranoutre	21/05/1917	28/05/1917
War Diary	Bailleul	29/05/1917	31/05/1917
War Diary	Magilligan Camp Bailleul	01/06/1917	10/06/1917
War Diary	St Jeans Capell	11/06/1917	22/06/1917
War Diary	Dranoutre	23/06/1917	29/06/1917
War Diary	Menis	30/06/1917	06/07/1917
War Diary	Wisernes	07/07/1917	31/07/1917
War Diary	Popperinge	01/08/1917	03/08/1917
War Diary	Mersey Camp	04/08/1917	17/08/1917
War Diary	Winnezeele	18/08/1917	24/08/1917
War Diary	Barastre	25/08/1917	30/08/1917
War Diary	Ytres	21/08/1917	30/11/1917
War Diary	Achiet Le Petit Lechelle	01/12/1917	01/12/1917
War Diary	Lechelle	02/12/1917	03/12/1917
War Diary	Sow G Grand	04/12/1917	16/12/1917
War Diary	Lucheux	17/12/1917	31/12/1917

War Diary	Corbie	01/01/1918	03/01/1918
War Diary	Coutre	04/01/1918	06/01/1918
War Diary	Harbonnieres	07/01/1918	12/01/1918
War Diary	Nesle	13/01/1918	14/01/1918
War Diary	Ollezy	15/01/1918	31/03/1918
War Diary	Gamaches	01/04/1918	08/04/1918
War Diary	Canal Bank Ypres	09/04/1918	12/04/1918
War Diary	Dragon Camp	13/04/1918	26/04/1918
War Diary	X Camp	27/04/1918	29/04/1918
War Diary	La Lovie	29/04/1918	30/04/1918
War Diary	La Lovie Chateau	01/05/1918	08/05/1918
War Diary	Couthove Chateau	09/05/1918	19/05/1918
War Diary	Couthove	20/05/1918	31/05/1918
War Diary	Couthove Chateau	01/06/1918	02/07/1918
War Diary	Cassell	03/07/1918	08/07/1918
War Diary	Terdeghem	09/07/1918	13/07/1918
War Diary	For 14th read 15	14/07/1918	14/07/1918
War Diary	For 15 read 14th	15/07/1918	22/07/1918
War Diary	Terdeghem	23/07/1918	28/08/1918
War Diary	St Sylvestre Capelle	01/09/1918	01/09/1918
War Diary	Eecke	02/09/1918	02/09/1918
War Diary	Mont Des Cats	03/09/1918	05/09/1918
War Diary	St Jeans Capell	06/09/1918	20/09/1918
War Diary	St Jeans & Biezen	21/09/1918	27/09/1918
War Diary	Vogeltje	28/09/1918	29/09/1918
War Diary	Ypres	30/09/1918	30/09/1918
War Diary	Ypres Ramparts	01/10/1918	01/10/1918
War Diary	Junction Camp St Jean	02/10/1918	14/10/1918
War Diary	Becelaere	15/10/1918	16/10/1918
War Diary	Ledeghem	17/10/1918	18/10/1918
War Diary	Lendelede	19/10/1918	28/10/1918
War Diary	Belleghem	29/10/1918	04/11/1918
War Diary	Mouscron	05/11/1918	24/03/1919

W095/24951 A3

36TH DIVISION
DIVL TROOPS

ASST DIR. VETY SERVICES
OCT 1915-MAR 1919

12/7432

36th/5 Western

Hq. 36th Division
A.S.T.S.
Vol I

Oct 15
Mar 1 . 19

Army Form C. 2118

WAR DIARY
or
INTELLIGENCE SUMMARY.
(Erase heading not required.)

Instructions regarding War Diaries and Intelligence Summaries are contained in F. S. Regs., Part II. and the Staff Manual respectively. Title pages will be prepared in manuscript.

Place	Date	Hour	Summary of Events and Information	Remarks and references to Appendices
Bordon	1/10/15	a.m.	Inspected the following Units — 48th Mobile Vety Sec — Field Ambulance Corps — Sid Cov & Reserve Park —	
		p.m.	Attended inspection by Inspector of Remounts — Inspected a horse of Mil Mob'le Sec Sid by by Inspector Stamp — Examined same, reported to D.D.V.S. a Mob'le Veterinary re precaution re mange. The Unit left for France following morning —	
	2/10/15	a.m.	Inspected Section Bot[tle]oy from LOC leaving — no other suspicious cases	
	3/10/15	a.m.	Visited office & see all packed up — handed OC Mobile Tramway [car] A.S.V.D. above re seeing everything away —	
		p.m.	Left Liphook — arrived Boulogne 10.30 pm	
	4/10/15	a.m.	Motored from Boulogne to Amettes with 4th QMG Section this Army.	
FLESSELLES	5/10/15	a.m.	Visited 2nd Corps & 3 Army H.Q. Nt Q. Nt Nobes Langford & the D.D.V.S. obtained instructions as returned etc to be arrested.	
		p.m.	Inspected lines of Mr M.P. was suppd or wtt D.V.S. Veg bad — nf 2 obtained — finds lands polluted — list reserve —	
	6/10/15	a.m.	Inspected 1/1 Can 70 Brigade at St SAUVEUR — horses supply good, W. Emph reg necessy	

1577 Wt.W10791/1773 500,000 1/15 D. D. & L. A.D.S.S./Forms/C. 2118.

WAR DIARY or INTELLIGENCE SUMMARY

Army Form C. 2118

Place	Date	Hour	Summary of Events and Information	Remarks and references to Appendices
FLESSELLES	6/7/15	a.m.	Ann Rations for horses not arriving properly — Condition of animal food — Instructed V.O. re duties & returns.	
	7/7/15	a.m.	Inspected the following units — M. to 20 Brigade at VILLERS BOCAGE — Camp satisfactory — habits suff^t good — Condition of animal food satisfactory — Condition Animals & artificers — 108. Field Ambulance at RUBEMPRE — habits suff^t, Condition Animals & artificers do do — 122. Field Coy R.E. at MIRVAUX — do do	
		p.m.	Inspected h.Q^rs 20 Coy A.S.C. at MOLLIENS AU BOIS do do — Inspected photoelectric Unit arrived at morning — Camp & billets satisfactory — Visited Camp of 15th Div 20 Brigade at ARGOEUVES — Camp satisfactory & units types food, hut alarm troughs much needed to prevent animals entering etc standing in mud — Instructed V.O. re duties & returns etc	
	8/7/15	a.m.	Inspection 2nd by A.S.C. at COISY with satisfactory results — 109 Field Ambulance at BERTANGLES do do — 150 Coy R.E. at do do — Instructed O.C. Mobile veterinary hospital at — Buffles a Det Ordre re sending horses to hospital — Reports to him that 2 horses had been left at tramway front in — LONGEAU	

1577 Wt.W10791/1773 500,000 1/15 D.D. & L. A.D.S.S./Forms/C. 2118.

WAR DIARY or INTELLIGENCE SUMMARY

Army Form C. 2118

Place	Date	Hour	Summary of Events and Information	Remarks and references to Appendices
PLESSELLES	9/10/15	a.m.	Rearranged details of VIIth Army & the move of the 11th Inf Brigade to 4th & 48th Divl areas for training — Visited HIGNACOURT & inspected 110th Field Ambulance	
Do	10/10/15	a.m.	Inspected details advancing from Cdts of 11th Bde R.E. at St SAUVEUR & ½ No II RA at VILLERS BOCAGE — Visited LONGEAU & inspected two teams left by 51st Amm Col. to NAMERVILLE — found not Lieut-Heavy ½ Bde had not received his Brigade order & getting no instructions. He failed to cite but both the others not having been in a town since the move — Sent Heavy of troops in a Car.	
Do	11/10/15	a.m.	D.D.V.S. 3rd Army came in — Inspected the Mobile Vet. Hos. little feed exception to the Water Supply & Bill the 9th horses which was very bad. An attempt was afterwards made to filled it — There was not sufficient water in the wells but what I I called the turns. The Pioneer Battalion & I Field Coy R.E. moved during the night out of the Rest Area — Reported the move to the troops — Inspected the 1/3rd Bde R.F.A. Water Supply & Horse artefacts — a number of isolated cases of ringworm are occurring.	
Do	12/10/15			

WAR DIARY
or
INTELLIGENCE SUMMARY.
(Erase heading not required.)

Army Form C. 2118

Place	Date	Hour	Summary of Events and Information	Remarks and references to Appendices
FLESSELLES	13/7/15	a.m	Inspected Out lines bil. at BERTY. — A number of poor horse owners, Company of good food but a little cramped, showing cleanliness, boot tops splendid. but arrangements for watering very unsatisfactory — Horses being watered from buckets — so to be — a number of horses cannot be watered in this manner. Again the need of canvas water troughs is apparent — A number of cases of neck sores & bow Creed — Some of these evidently neglected by friction from the Brie pad. Wh. others again appear chin lice to be apparent.	
			Visited Kappe-en-sol. Saw over my Convoy in form of acne. Inspected R.T.O. at Railhead re evacuation of sick — Appears to be routed to clearing of army in Motile lie from Hd Qrs lo by Railhead — Watering lots of the guides re Catting arrangements in Trucks & recommended that canvas troughs be used for	
Do	16/7/15	a.m	Inspected 46th Hants Brigade at VAUX EN AMIENOIS — Condition of horses and general cleanliness — Boot tops place & watering arrangements unsatisfactory — Horses troughs are in the process of being made — L.D. Horse and Battery 10th Hy & Battery being added by local purchase — a trial that horses	

WAR DIARY
or
INTELLIGENCE SUMMARY.
(Erase heading not required.)

Army Form C. 2118

Instructions regarding War Diaries and Intelligence Summaries are contained in F. S. Regs., Part II. and the Staff Manual respectively. Title pages will be prepared in manuscript.

Place	Date	Hour	Summary of Events and Information	Remarks and references to Appendices
PLESSELLES u/s (continued)			Fuels have being slipped - made a note of having an extra published - a few cases of stomach worm occurring - wrote at my billets to Pet Purchase Executive of forage of the year - that 10lbs hay was not sufficient for horses of the LD type & that the remaining 2lbs should be made up Bouteat - Bran & Bean [ones?] should be given as an additional or not substitution diet.	
Do	15-16/75	A.m.	Inspected HdQrs Staff Horses, Bat Reg't C₃ & 303 By Add - arrangements satisfactory excepting the water supply which cannot be remedied - however the sickness or rickness are occurring to lean animal of drinking this stagnant water & the horses been be sent to cold relief. Received wire from A.D.V.S. veterinary reporting a serious outbreak of mange in the 'B' Brigade R.A. - whole section moved to Railhead.	
		P.m.	Visited 149Q, 108th Inf Brigade at MOLLIENS AU BOIS - inspected 253 Coy A.S.C. & the 108th Field Ambulance	

WAR DIARY
or
INTELLIGENCE SUMMARY.

(Erase heading not required.)

Army Form C. 2118

Place	Date	Hour	Summary of Events and Information	Remarks and references to Appendices
FLESSELLES	16/5	pm.	Drove over to the Hd Quarters of the 1/2nd Bde R.A. in the 08th Div. area at SAILLY in connection with a line ordered programme. Returned to THIEVRES where the horses were in camp & battery over the western side the road found the Ned 35 trees on hand with several of very violent type - supplied this evening the A.D.V.S. Lieutenant the permanent cases —	
Do	18/5	am.	Inspected Veterinary Section — Visited camp of 1/13 Bde R.A. at ARQUEVES & 115 Bde R.A. at ST. SAUVEUR also Bde Ammunition Column at BRETUY. Did not make an inspection but observed nature of work & took to Us.	
Do	19/5	am.	Drove over to HENU in the 37 Bde Div area at that opportunity of the Bds. S. to whom non medical attention being carried out by them today, by the new intra-dermal palpebral method — spent a most instructive morning & cases of mange much improved by the rapidity & simplicity of the method. 9 cases of mange reported from the Bde Ammunition Column — Re allotted duties of V.Os. consequent on the move of the 1/3 & 1/4 Mdn Bde. R.J.R. to the front line & the return of the 1/2 & 1/2 Mdn Bde.	

WAR DIARY or INTELLIGENCE SUMMARY

Army Form C. 2118

Place	Date	Hour	Summary of Events and Information	Remarks and references to Appendices
PLESSIEL	20/10	am	Visited HENU to see the results of the rabbit inoculations — the one cet is typical reactions — the one cat that reacted could be gotten was not marked	
		pm	Visited Mobile Sec at Rolland & 51st Ann. Column at BREILLY. Made full enquiries at the latter place re the mange cases. Suspects two cases that had been evacuated to the Mobile Section. Arranged for Mycetic smears with inoculations — The column moves tomorrow to the 33rd Corps —	
Do	21/10	am	Visited HENU to see post-mortem on reactor. Inspected H.M.P. horses in PLESSIEL area. evacuated 3 to the Mobile Sec. Recommended 2 or 3 others should be replaced as unsuitable —	
		pm	Visited 51st Ann. Col. again to inspect horses picked out by O.C. Mobile at his inspection as itchy — No leaves of mange in any of them. Placed the whole section in working rotation — loaned Boots & Syringe etc that at camp of 51st Ann. Column to places as by hounds for the incoming Division.	
Do	22/10	am	Division moved to new area with Head Quarters at DOMART EN PONTHIEU. Intended to Mobile to evacuate all cases left behind & move horses	

1577 Wt. W10791/1773 500,000 1/15 D. D. & L. A.D.S.S./Forms/C. 2118.

Army Form C. 2118.

WAR DIARY
or
INTELLIGENCE SUMMARY.
(Erase heading not required.)

Instructions regarding War Diaries and Intelligence Summaries are contained in F.S. Regs., Part II. and the Staff Manual respectively. Title pages will be prepared in manuscript.

Place	Date	Hour	Summary of Events and Information	Remarks and references to Appendices
FLESSELLES (continued)	22nd	10 a.m.	Mr Ruthead on the 21st inst. On my way to DOMART I called & see a/m left behind by 107th Brigade in VIGNACOURT suffering from pneumonia — found them very bad — sent they both [illegible] for some time —	
DOMART	23rd	10 a.m.	Visited MONTRELET. On arriving saw Sgt. Sgt. Brown & asked me to [illegible]. Along with the M.O. the hospital & fitted a car to Evac. Coy on leaving FLESSELLES. Visited to/8th Bde H.Q. guide at BEAUVAL - saw the O.C. Left 2 evacuated men here to Casualties. Visited BERNEUIL to billeting area of 9th Lin. Rde R.F. & called on the Bryson Junior Capt lat V.O.	
D	24 15	10 a.m.	Received mention of indents for treatment & to ascertain that same will be expeditiously expedited & late arrivals be attended to between the Bns. Meetings. Visited CANAPLES & complete to temps for Brit. Arms divisions 9/15/en Bde R.F.A. I was a great pleasure [illegible] in the Cattle hurt — Popes also not being taken & evacuated — the V.O. being a both experience of anything — boxes at the new cones at Call Supply in this neighbourhood very good — De Fairlin Co. Captain of [illegible] of troops	

1577 Wt. W10791/1773 500,000 1/15 D. D. & L. A.D.S.S./Forms/C. 2118.

WAR DIARY
or
INTELLIGENCE SUMMARY.
(Erase heading not required.)

Army Form C. 2118

Place	Date	Hour	Summary of Events and Information	Remarks and references to Appendices
DOMART	25/10/15	a.m.	Visited Hd Quar's of Brig Gen Thin & talk with him re – He informed me of 2 horses he had left behind at Bertangles which had not been evacuated. Visited DOULLENS & inspected the 18th horses in their new billets – have an stable & sheds to accommodate about 40 animals – The situation is cool & the men comfortable.	
Do	26/10/15	p.m.	Again visited DOULLENS to arrange for the distribution of a batch of Remounts which arrived this morning.	
Do	27/10/15	a.m.	Inspected the sites of the Camps of the A.S.C. Coys at MONTRELET – Sites of No 1 Coy bad, too flat & muddy, no proper drainage – have supplied Sand – Rest of the horses out at work so arranged to inspect them later. Visited Font-Bialet in Two Pierres – unable to fix a day for some days – And – Next Moment at Hd Qur.s G.O.C. 51st Div when consulted him re arranging for next Bidules.	
Do	28/10/15	a.m.	Arranged to look after all Remount Horses myself, including the 36" 51st Arty Coys & Remounts – unable to ascertain one horse from disregard by Pty Loy & Remount – spoke with BOYS on the telephone re returns.	

WAR DIARY
or
INTELLIGENCE SUMMARY.
(Erase heading not required.)

Army Form C. 2118.

Place	Date	Hour	Summary of Events and Information	Remarks and references to Appendices
DOMART	29/5	a.m.	Visited Hd Quarters of 108th Infy Brigade at RIBEAUCOURT, also Battalions at FIENVILLERS & BERNAVILLE – Sar Sgt Church a.v.c. asked me to inspect one or two horses – Examined 1 Horse from 30th Ryl Irish Cey with amputated eye & 1 horse from 13 R.I.R. for debility – Forwarded a supplementary indent for Remounts.	
Do	30/5	a.m.	Office work.	
		p.m.	Visited 107th Infy Brigade Hd Quarters at CANAPLES – Sar Sgt Hillard a.v.c. & several sick things were found on	
Do	31/5	a.m.	Visited tub troops inspected the first cavalry at ST HILAIRE – Horses all under shelter in barns etc – Condition good – Lots of hay & food & no complaints about forage.	

Nov 15

WAR DIARY
or
INTELLIGENCE SUMMARY

Army Form C. 2118.

Place	Date	Hour	Summary of Events and Information	Remarks and references to Appendices
DOMART	1/5	p.m.	Inspected 3rd train R.E. at MONTRELET — Horses all under cover others condition very good — A noticeable difference in the condition of animals which had recently been returned from hospital, these being much poorer. Shoeing good. All horses drawing rations on the 30 lb/day/head scale — No reason to speak to the V.O. concerning his condition on parade, being too keen to get drunk — Also reported this matter to this O.C. & asked him to inform me if there were any further trouble of [unclear] sort.	
	2/5	a.m.	Visited DOULLENS tramways for the distribution of animals.	
	3/5		Visited 75th Bde R.F.A. at HEM — Inspected site of camp which was a very bad one on a new ploughed mud — Reported matter to O.C. & advised changing the site to higher ground. Visited Yorkshire R.A. at BONNEVILLE & inspected the horses of 2 batteries which have been losing well cared for. No V.O. employed, that being allowed to purchase locally when none available.	
	4/5		Ordered to send a V.O. between 22nd Division & stores, Lieut. BIDLAKE to proceed forthwith.	
	5/5	a.m.	Went to MONTRELET to interview Requisitioning Officer re local purchase of hay.	

Army Form C. 2118.

WAR DIARY
or
INTELLIGENCE SUMMARY
(Erase heading not required.)

Instructions regarding War Diaries and Intelligence Summaries are contained in F. S. Regs., Part II. and the Staff Manual respectively. Title pages will be prepared in manuscript.

Place	Date	Hour	Summary of Events and Information	Remarks and references to Appendices
DOMART	5th/15	(contd.)	Arranged with Remount Officer that untrained horses should be allowed to further really themselves through him. Sam LIEUT BIDLAKE instructions re going 22nd Divn to drive him to LONGHEAU to catch his train.	
		6.15 am	Inspected 1/2 Lon Fd Bde at BERNEUIL — All horses led by General indication of horses good — showing satisfaction — troops & horses in hand & strained by visiting immediately the Brigade arrived in this country.	
		7.15 am	Inspected 1/3 Bn Fd Bde at HEM — all horses led by — General condition good, especially two teams — 9th Batty had largest number of poor horses showing not up to date — troops have not been able to obtain its right site for camp being changed on my advice & now recuperating. Arranged to forward horse as an H.O. also invented CO's charger, & vet returns — Fat good stables for sick lines. Billyarm now in hand & an improvement shown in grooming with the division. In calm 2ho d'bay not being made up by local purchase. Brigade would like more bran otherwise [?] absolutely stresses in lieu of body brushes	

1577 Wt. W10791/1773 500,000 1/15 D. D. & L. A.D.S.S./Forms/C. 2118.

WAR DIARY
or
INTELLIGENCE SUMMARY
(Erase heading not required.)

Army Form C. 2118.

Place	Date	Hour	Summary of Events and Information	Remarks and references to Appendices
DOMART		8.15 am	Inspected 11th Bn F.A. Brigade - Horses lively - Condition very satisfactory - especially 103 Batty. - Shoeing not up to date. Regime more time & linseed - All animals under shelter - but troughs food & watering stream - Rugs not in use.	
		9.15	Inspected 105th Field Ambulance Coy horses - Horses 2 & up ago 1 month this division still damp feet - Condition of horses good throughout but site (?) the western division - Billets at BERTAUCOURT.	
			Inspected 108th Field Ambulance at HOUDENCOURT - Horses not under shelter but site & camp good - Shoeing up to date - No skin disease.	
			Visited head quarters 4th/4th H Bde re hallowing of horses for battery about to leave the Division. Inspected transport animals of D.H.Q. & Sussex Regt. at BEAUVAL - Found case of Ringworm - Evacuated 1 horse & 1 mule for D.Vety reserve - Inspected animals of 10th Bat R. Irish Fus. (numbered 2 H.D.'s & 1 Mule for Vety reserve - Inspected animals of 9th Bat R. Irish Fus. at GEZAINCOURT - Found half the animal teams de-roostat with cracked heels, suppurating wounds about the coronet etc. - Evacuated 27 to hospital - See hospital & sent in special report to Brit./Hosp. Vety.	

Army Form C. 2118.

WAR DIARY
or
INTELLIGENCE SUMMARY.
(Erase heading not required.)

Instructions regarding War Diaries and Intelligence Summaries are contained in F.S. Regs., Part II and the Staff Manual respectively. Title pages will be prepared in manuscript.

Place	Date	Hour	Summary of Events and Information	Remarks and references to Appendices
DOMART	11/15		Attended inspection by D.D.R. 3rd Army of Animals of No 1 Horse Stn for Canada starting — Animals found shorn up. Orders to 2 batteries leaving for overseas sent in fortnight order for Remounts	
	12/1/15	am		
		pm	Inspected transport animals & all Equipments of 19th Infantry Brigade. Condition very satisfactory. Found 1 LD horse & 1 tongs drawn Regt: & vices & unable to do his job in a reasonable number waggon.	
	13/1/15	am	Inspected 10th Batt: Royal Irish Lan: Col. at CANADIEES. Found camp & horses in a deplorable state. Animals standing up to fetlocks in liquid muck & far too few any used. Animals wretched & evidently starved. Reported matter to D.O.C. Div. Comd: & highest with C.R.A. Comm.	
	14/1/15	am	Inspected R.A.C. with the C.R.A. — Picked out all the worst animals & had them put on on a site for special treatment. — Numbers as follows — No 1 See — Horses 51 Mules 20 — No 2 do Horses 58 Mules 14 — No 3 See Horses 86 Mules 42. The latter section by far the worst.	

WAR DIARY
or
INTELLIGENCE SUMMARY.
(Erase heading not required.)

Army Form C. 2118.

Place	Date	Hour	Summary of Events and Information	Remarks and references to Appendices
DUNKIRK	14ᵗʰ (continued)		Decided that no 3 tee in tents are under shelter. No. 2 tent affairs are longer than static management — Personnel extra feeding routine	
	15ᵗʰ/15			
	16/15	a.m	Visited Rothery to see & arrange for despatch of no Remount	
	17/15	p.m	Visited Remount to see Proview Petrerion Canadian Depot depots, recruit town under the administration of ten 36ᵗʰ Divn. Inspected transport animals & found all arrangements excellent — Arranges for Veg. allowances etc.	
	18/15	a.m	Office	
		p.m	Leave & Inspect Remount of 82ⁿᵈ Divn. just received. Inc. called two D/horses — 1 C for fines to store — ten fried foot hocks & dead lame real back — 1 HD. 18 mare lame near for for Ringbone Ridestro	
	19/15	a.m	Inspected Transport animals of 2ⁿᵈ Rest Camp Pro at MENVILLERS — Yes (and Caseteria — Inspected 1 Pack pony — Hampered 1 Mephon Whale (pones) to 14 S.S.T.R.R.R.	
		p.m	Visited mobile v. Rail head	

WAR DIARY or INTELLIGENCE SUMMARY

Army Form C. 2118.

Place	Date	Hour	Summary of Events and Information	Remarks and references to Appendices
DOMART	20/5	am	ADVS 3rd Army came over about the question of ADVS Sergeants & farriers generally.	
		pm	Insp. ADV S 3rd Army at MONTRELET (Hd Qrs 3rd Div Train) He came over to inspect some horses for casting for Remount Reserve.	
	21/5	am	ADVS 3rd Army inspected 15 Bat Amm Column in consequence of my adverse report. He ordered the evacuation of 45 horses & made it the most of the debilitated animals.	
	22/5	am	Inspected horses of 108th Field Ambulance at HOUDENCOURT – All were over tired and ill.	
		pm	Inspected Mobile Vet. Section Just. LIEUT. CONNOCHIE who has just been posted to this division – Instructed him to CAMAPLES & posted him to the 15th Bn Amm Col.	
	23/5	am	Inspected 12th Field Coy R.E. just returned to Bat. 245 from ARQUEVES. Animals in good condition after being in the open.	
		pm	Visited Mobile Veterinary the disposal of Orne Remounts – Ordered destruction of 2 horses 1/6 1/5 T.A. Bde suffering from villitis	
	24/5	am	Visited L'ETOILE to select a site for the Mobile Vet. & our Overseers	

WAR DIARY or INTELLIGENCE SUMMARY

Army Form C. 2118.

Place	Date	Hour	Summary of Events and Information	Remarks and references to Appendices
DOMART	24th (Continued)		No stabling available (recommended) - the required number of animals.	
	25/3/15	a.m.	Visited 112th Bde at BERNEUIL (inspect arm horses - Gallenee 5 horses suffering from strangles, one of which showed ulceration of the Schneiderian membrane & mouth, but none others were shedding. Did not expect reactions - had them done more as a demonstration of the mew latest dermopalpebral method.	
		p.m.	Visited Aid Amm Col. & instructed the V.O. re returns etc.	
	26/3/15	a.m.	Inspected animals of 109th Field Ambulances at BEAUVAL - Condition of animals very good, stable management good. The O.S. is a first horse.	
			Inspected animals of 11 Batt R. train Two at CANDAS - Amount looking well specially the mules - a very fine lot of horses Transport Officer - this battalion has about plenty of H.Q. horse.	
	27/3/15	a.m.	Visited (7 & 15th Gee Un rewett) relieving the horses - 2 have sore distinct reactions - Called (via full report from the V.O. - 2 of these horses showed Copious Nasal discharge from both nostrils & also some on face	

1577 Wt.W10791/1773 500,000 1/15 D.D. & L. A.D.S.S./Forms/C. 2118.

WAR DIARY
or
INTELLIGENCE SUMMARY.
(Erase heading not required.)

Army Form C. 2118.

Place	Date	Hour	Summary of Events and Information	Remarks and references to Appendices
DOMART	27/15	(September)	Surface alteration of the Television Operations, but when last seen served from one of them, there was little to be seen on the underlying membrane. Orders then onwards to be kept in isolation & selected by intravenous method after theatre of area. Visits HOUDENCOURT & St HILAIRE giving instructions re the turning of approach with civilians.	
	28/15	am	Saw the whole of the 11th Bn 20 Ble proceed by a stirring traverse. Horses looking entering well. Whole sow sick animals — horses looking poor & run down — helps on Task turned out — horses disfigured. 2d We than moved to PONTREMY — went to LONGPRE to meet reinforcements.	
	29/15	am		
PONTREMY	30/15	am	Visited Mobile See at L'ETOILE — Visited DUNEQ, LIAUCOURT, FRANCIERES & BELLANCOURT. I found a more suitable place in the latter — found billet site at the latter place which was about 1 mile from ABBEVILLE & have will therefore be able to be evacuated by road	

Ask. 36/2 str.
bot: 3

121/1928

WAR DIARY or INTELLIGENCE SUMMARY

Army Form C. 2118.

Place	Date	Hour	Summary of Events and Information	Remarks and references to Appendices
PONTREMY	1/12/15		Visited 153rd Bde R.A. at LONG, met the V.O. (LIEUT PAUL) & instructed him re returns etc – Visited 172nd Bde R.A. at BOUCHON and the V.O. (LIEUT SHAW) instructing him likewise, also the 173rd Bde R.A. at VAUCHELLES meeting the V.O. (CAPT. McCLINTOCK) – 156th Bde R.A. not yet arrived.	
do	2/12/15	a.m.	Visited the 3 Vet Hospital at ABBEVILLE	
		p.m.	Received wire from D.D.V.S. & Army stating that I have of the 1/2 Lon. Bde R.A. transmitted to Lieutenant on the 28th who had given a faulty reaction to mallein at the Base – Visited 1/2 Bde at FRANKVILLE & & & Portendre about the horse – Inspected 5 horses of 1/2 Bde in Isolation which were listed at BERNEVIL & an protest reactions – 3 animals showing suspicious symptoms – 4 of the 5 horse are from "C" Sub sec 1/5 "B" Batty & 1 from A Sub sec. The horse which reacted at the Base was from "B" Sub sec. of mature of the horses. No reactions as far as in any of the animals.	
do	3/12/15		Visited 1/2 Bde & gave Later result of Patrick's inoculation of the horses. No reactions as far as in any of the animals.	

WAR DIARY or INTELLIGENCE SUMMARY

Army Form C. 2118.

Place	Date	Hour	Summary of Events and Information	Remarks and references to Appendices
PONTREMY	4/2/15	a.m.	Visited FRANKVILLE again. Re result of mallein inoculation – no local reaction – A.D.V.S. 3rd Army came to see the horses – destroyed all five.	
	5/2/15		Found all to be affected apart mortem. Visited Mobile Vet Sec. at BELLANCOURT – inspected sea stables – Found everything satisfactory – mallein'd 2 horses suspect – have moved on - no patent reaction by the 27th inoculum.	
	6/2/15	a.m.	Visited ½ Mob to inspect in 4 & 5 Cav batteries mallein'd yesterday. Found no typical reaction – advised in inoculating the remainder of the Brigade. Received intimation from A.D.V.S. 3rd Army that 2 glandered horses had been destroyed at BOUCHON.	
		p.m.	A.D.V.S. 32nd Div. came over to see me re the glandered horse destroyed at BOUCHON – saw our own horses viewed by A.D.S.S. & ½ Mob for the latter move – 2 of them horses were badly affected with mange. Called on a report.	
	7/2/15	a.m.	Inspected the 2 horses mallein'd in the 5 & 6th inst. – no reaction. Visited ½ Mob to inspect mallein'd horses.	

1577 Wt. W10791/1773 500,000 1/15 D. D. & L. A.D.S.S./Forms/C. 2118.

WAR DIARY
or
INTELLIGENCE SUMMARY.
(Erase heading not required.)

Army Form C. 2118.

Place	Date	Hour	Summary of Events and Information	Remarks and references to Appendices
PONT REMY	7/12/15	a.m.	Office — Visit from C.R.A. & Farrier — Walked to COQUEREL to see N.C.O. of 154th Bde R.A. (Lieut Miller) & give him instructions re relieving the sick	
do	8/12/15		Spent the day at FRANKVILLE — destroyed 1 horse which reacted during last 5 months — 5 patched reactors evacuated to Mob Vet. Sec. — visited DOMART — inspected horses of M.M.P. 13th Corps — evacuated 2 inj. (injured?) horses. I have visited LONG — rechecked 60 horses there by a.s.r. — None had been withdrawn from the infected area	
do	9/12/15			
do	10/12/15	a.m.	Inspected hulleinen horses of No 1 Coy A.S.C. — no reactors — Went to see the V.O.'s of 172nd Bde & 173rd Bde — Arranged to remove hulleining 173 Bde on Sunday next	
		p.m.	Office — Re allotted duties of V.O.s every to the expansion of the territorial artillery on the 11th & 12th instant — forwarded final report on outbreak of glanders — 1/3 hr (?) from Belg. R.A.	
11/12/15		a.m.	Inspected hulleinen horses of No 1 Coy A.S.C. — No reactors — visited his Comdt at FRANSU reported to V.O. re new visited ABBEVILLE to exchange trellein	

Army Form C. 2118.

WAR DIARY
or
INTELLIGENCE SUMMARY.
(Erase heading not required.)

Instructions regarding War Diaries and Intelligence Summaries are contained in F. S. Regs., Part II. and the Staff Manual respectively. Title pages will be prepared in manuscript.

Place	Date	Hour	Summary of Events and Information	Remarks and references to Appendices
PONTREMY	12/75	a.m.	T. Artillery entraining. Examined all horses of "A" Battle Div Am Col also 1 of 13 & 4 of C Bat Lee on account Influenza cases Amongst Unit have been reported recently. With a view to clearing out every animal in any way suspicious also all private contacts.	
	13/75	a.m.	Visited 173 Bde at VAUCHELLES. Commenced inoculating — Visited	
		p.m.	Artillery School at HAVERNAS. & few 3 Section — 16 Officers & 01 & NCOs	
	14/75	a.m.	Inspected influenza horses of 173 Bde — no reactions — Condition of animals very good.	
	15/75	p.m.	Visited Vet Hospital & the Major Holden Jarrett for Hosening. Visited VAUCHELLES, MOUFLERS & VILLERS SOUS AILLY & Inspect Influenzd	
		a.m.	Arrived 173 Bde. Inspected Horses in Am. Col. Condition of animals of Am Col. not so good as the remainder of the Brigade	
	16/75	p.m.	This — Went to Recked after tea to meet Removents.	
		a.m.	Again Inspected Influenza animals 173 Bde — Inoculation reactors of Mobile Section for reacting — Visited Mobile Section	
	16/15		& commented influenza horses of No 1 Coy Asc — no reactions.	

WAR DIARY or INTELLIGENCE SUMMARY

Army Form C. 2118.

Place	Date	Hour	Summary of Events and Information	Remarks and references to Appendices
PONTREMY	17/5	am	Visited Inds Vet Sec to meet DDR 3 Army & discuss up some lines for crating. Handed in programme for relieving all Units after Boro – spoke to DDVS re the printed instructions for relieving stock. Are impossible to carry out with reference to the times for inspecting after sweeten, then dung to large numbers of animals & at different places. He agreed & then suggested that it could possibly be seen them at the 20th & 25th hours.	
	18/5	am	Visited L'ETOILE Evacuated "suspect" animals suffering from cracked heels & where Vet S.A.C. Evacuated 30 animals & destroyed 3 – destroyed a special report to Sir W.B.95 concerning the state of affairs.	
	19/5	am	Office – Visited Mobile V.S. re permanent standings & veterinary programme.	
	20/5	7am	Visited BOUCHON & antsta in the relieving of the 172nd Bde.	
		1pm	Office – Issued instructions re Evacuation & dealing with sick in the event of an emergency move.	
	21/5	am	Inspected billeted horses of 172nd RFA & CA – 1 heelers & Salt-ordered exercise list in exercise	
		pm	Went to hospital (Tel. Needles & Sharepads).	

Army Form C. 2118.

WAR DIARY
or
INTELLIGENCE SUMMARY.
(Erase heading not required.)

Instructions regarding War Diaries and Intelligence Summaries are contained in F. S. Regs., Part II. and the Staff Manual respectively. Title pages will be prepared in manuscript.

Place	Date	Hour	Summary of Events and Information	Remarks and references to Appendices
PONT REMY	22/12/15	am	Visited Mob. Vet. Sec. Inspected mallenied horses of 1st Mobile, also 9th R.E. Two of 12th Field Coy R.E. — No serious condition of all animals inspected.	
		pm	Inspected a batten of 61st Sup Coy — Horses all under cover & arrangements good.	
	23/12/15	am	Visited BOUCHON & LONG. Inspected mallenied horses. Horse of C. Batt 172 Bde at BOUCHON recently fired [shot] in both eyes — destroyed & post mortem. Only one typical nodule could be found. Several fibrous nodules, ? of recent nos. 1 Patient heart in Amm Col 172 Bde — Ordered cooked. Rest in field-ease [?]	
		pm	Visited SURCAMPS. Inspected mallenied horses of Army Cyclist. No reactors.	
	24/12/15	am	Visited 172 Bde. Inspected Patient heart of khum Col. Simular reaction in control eye — Not much problem, but no jaw move prevent muchenye — Examined him have been Mobile Vet. Sec. In isolating.	
	25/12/15	am	Visited Mobile. Inspected Patient heart from horse at 172 Bde — horse mallied [?] in control eye (ie on 2nd day) — (movies from no reaction — Ordered cooked. Patent noted. Inspected Ichnoptic Amm Col at LIERCOURT & BLONDELLE — animals in good condition for ?: [?]	

1577 Wt.W10791/1773 500,000 1/15 D. D. & L. A.D.S.S./Forms/C. 2118.

Army Form C. 2118.

WAR DIARY
or
INTELLIGENCE SUMMARY.
(Erase heading not required.)

Place	Date	Hour	Summary of Events and Information	Remarks and references to Appendices
PONT REMY	27/5	am	Visited L'ÉTOILE & reported to Recovery Hosp. & Div Amm Col — Visited Mobile Vet Sec. & hove of Amm Col 72nd Bde — tested contents — disinfected vesicles. Visited FRANKVILLE for hot but infected area vacated by H.Q. Don't Bde was for specs placarded — found all correct — Visited Rotating School at WAVERNAS & detailed to Offrs' Class 2 to 3 pm, NCOs 3 to 4 pm.	
	28/5		As inspected Influenza horse cases of D.A.C. Condition of mules very good indeed.	
		pm	Went to trouble to destroy planned horse of Amm Col 72nd Bde — SS.V.S. 3 Army came & see post mortem — Both lungs crammed full of tubercles.	
	29/5	am	Inspected influenza horses of 154th Bde R.F.A. — 3/o control lost in exercise. Condition general good — inspected horses of 153 Bde — No creations. Condition general good — 2 cases of suspected mange evacuated from 75 Batt 153 Bde.	
	30/5	am	Inspected own Amm/Pd wagons of 154th & 153 Bdes R.F.A. — Also inspected all advanced animals of B.A.C.	
		pm	Visited GORENFLOS & inspect a partial vacate of 15 Chauntier Inn.	

Army Form C. 2118.

WAR DIARY
or
INTELLIGENCE SUMMARY.
(Erase heading not required.)

Instructions regarding War Diaries and Intelligence Summaries are contained in F.S. Regs., Part II. and the Staff Manual respectively. Title pages will be prepared in manuscript.

Place	Date	Hour	Summary of Events and Information	Remarks and references to Appendices
PONT REMY	31/12/17	a.m.	Visited 153 D.I.S.E Brigades RFA. & the remounts of advertising — I heard from 153 A/She evacuated Mobile See as a patient reader — for a number of weeks — to treat in both eyes. N.E. Crickmonth resting, but ordered excess of discharge — forwarded to O.C. Mobile V. Elect Veterinary. Visited Mobile Vet. Sec. to see result of selecting 5 horses which were for test section from his 1/2 Bn Rifle Brigade — Rated by who decmn. half patrols— after an interval of 3 weeks — 2 positive Reactn — Orders cutaneous test to confirm. p.m. Visited 153 Ride Brigade RFA at FRANKVILLE & saw the VO in the front line — also visited FRANSU Stables & the D.A.C. Officer — Visited Field Park at 153 Div. Artillery at LONGVILLERS also the Mobile Vet. Sec the Personnel — V.O. was away at the time.	

1577 Wt. W10791/1773 500,000 1/15 D. D. & L. A.D.S.S./Forms/C. 2118.

Avis. 36½ öre
tot: 4

Tau > 16

WAR DIARY or INTELLIGENCE SUMMARY

Army Form C. 2118.

Place	Date	Hour	Summary of Events and Information	Remarks and references to Appendices
PONT REMY	1st		Visited P.V.S. transport horses of this Bde RA which had been reported as needing - also looked up some horses for invaliding to SDR.	
	2nd		Revised the mallein programme for the Division. Relegated 3 horses of this Bde Fd Art had reacted on retesting by the prophylactic & hypodermic methods - Some entered on post mortem. Two 3 days I Army were present at the post-mortems.	
	3rd		Rode to OC. wt Mules & CHAPLES Stables & sel- Visited No 5 Vety Hospital & Sgt-Mallier & Troops for testing 53rd Div Arty. Visited No 2 & 5 Sn 53rd Div Arty & arrange mallein-Testing. Also V.O team playing entertainment outfield within between Silesia - Sanatoria house for Lindston 4 & 10th insts & visit bulletin 15th & 16th insts.	
			Visited No 1 Ambulance rest at BETTENCOURT and the V.O. LIEUT DRINKWATER arranged for him transit LIEUT BARTRUM in mallein-testing ½ week	
	4th		Rde. Routine	

WAR DIARY
or
INTELLIGENCE SUMMARY.
(Erase heading not required.)

Army Form C. 2118.

Place	Date	Hour	Summary of Events and Information	Remarks and references to Appendices
DOMART	5/10	a.m.	Visited 1/2 hotel Res at FRANVILLERS - inspected horses - saw sections - American farm are here also. Dr Bentley shewed me drawings - Some Idaho Reptiles sent. Visited LONGVILLIERS & inspect waterment Horses of 34 hotch Res - no reaction. Visited HESNIL - DOMQUEUR & inspect some horses of the 11 hotch Res expect 100 available	
	6/10	a.m.	Visited GORBEVILLE & went to see the 60 westlinds Shewered half Grid Quarter & attention horses also the Syndicon but 1/2 fortnight indent for remounts - great trouble in 36th Div Artillery - sent in a report for the Guide & attend this. Inspected horses collected yesterday - Visited AILES MONT bivouac & collecting 1/4st Canadigonamen & saw impalment the horses & an expect return to them.	
	7/10	p.m.	Received a limit from DDVS 3 Army reporting 2 Remounts (horses 1 mule) that have lowered by 43rd M.V.S. that should reside to Anoleon at this Base. Am sent beloged to 36th Div Corn Col. Other horses to 153, 136. R.D.	

WAR DIARY
or
INTELLIGENCE SUMMARY.

(Erase heading not required.)

Army Form C. 2118.

Place	Date	Hour	Summary of Events and Information	Remarks and references to Appendices
DUMART	8/10	8 a.m.	Delivered 1 remount for H.Q.'s retention. Reported this down to "Z" and returned on dispatch car. A straggler horse to Mailhead to hand on tomorrow to the 53rd Div Artillery.	
		p.m.	Forwarded report form [Battalion] of the 2nd Army which remained Duellen at the time of the 53rd.	
	9/10	a.m.	Inspected sheltered horses. On doubtful mules watched – Directed the Cavalry at Sgt HILLMRIE to inspect a patrol remain. Ordered transfer to the Mobile for retention.	
		p.m.	Office	
	10/10	a.m.	Inspected sheltered horses & mules & horse of division to be Brought for retention. Visited BUXECOURT collecting half the animals of M. McCaughdon.	
		p.m.	Inspected horses for Artillery. McCutcheon's Pole – also a number of horses required to be exchanged as being draught.	
	11/10	a.m.	Succeeded exam of orange from the H.M.R. Inspected sheltered horses of M. Gaul & others – no retentions.	

WAR DIARY
or
INTELLIGENCE SUMMARY.
(Erase heading not required.)

Army Form C. 2118.

Instructions regarding War Diaries and Intelligence Summaries are contained in F.S. Regs., Part II and the Staff Manual respectively. Title pages will be prepared in manuscript.

Place	Date	Hour	Summary of Events and Information	Remarks and references to Appendices
DOMART	11/6	pm	Visited 153rd Bde re lectures & leaves. Arrived at Westmore. Sent Lt. Col. to Brigade. Also visited the 154th Bde and RWF S.O.	
	12/6	am	Inspected cookhouses of 1st Cameronians and received the remounts.	
		pm	Inspected hv. P. horses & remounts and the offenders. Horses all to be clipped out & remounts to stable night.	
	13/6	am	Inspected machine gun & Lewis gun inspection - Had to rearrange brigade detraining arrangements - Declined at Westleton's School MANGONIES	
		pm	2 to 4 pm	
	14/6	am	Inspected Cookhouses &c. of 6th Cameronians	
		pm	Visited MONTROUET to look at entrenchments etc for the Mobile	
	15/6	am	Inspected horses (1st Cantons) of the Welsh Brigade - Also inspected a battery & Army Col. Amunh - Good condition	
	16/6	am	Office	
		pm	Visited LONGUEVILLETTE (see 1 arrived place for the Mobile	
	17/6	pm	Head Qrs BETTENCOURT. Visited 2DR J Army. Also inspecting horses for troops.	

Army Form C. 2118.

WAR DIARY
or
INTELLIGENCE SUMMARY.
(Erase heading not required.)

Place	Date	Hour	Summary of Events and Information	Remarks and references to Appendices
DOMART BERNAVILLE	18/16	a.	Lt. Col. McQuade changes from DOMART to BERNAVILLE. Visited R.A. Head Quarters. Interview V/G arrangements. Transportation etc.	
			Visited after Artillery & this transp area at the Front. Visited M.V.S. at BELLANCOURT - gave instructions re rotating & toted Remits, also discussed more freewheel.	
	20/16	a.m	Inspected arm horses for casting of 53rd & 5th Damm. Bat. at FRANSU. Also visited & tested Bn. at FRANVILLE.	
	21/16	a.m	Inspected 36th Div Damm. Col. at ST OUEN. Sent in an inspection report for Hd Quarters and also for 5D2 Rt.	
		p.m	53rd ASC Inspected the animals & cart establishment - The contr: of all horses on malleins by A.S.T. system.	
	22/16	a.m.	Visited ANS Inspected (1) postal section relation Col. Mille 3, 154 Bde & 36th A.D. 3) Formed 3 suspicious cases - Ordered all to be tested by contact method.	
		p.m.	Visited LONGVILLERS & instructed N.O. to Mitchell Rate & malleining remainders of animals of 53rd Bde.	

1577 Wt.W10791/1773 500,000 1/15 D.D. & L. A.D.S.S./Forms/C. 2118.

WAR DIARY or INTELLIGENCE SUMMARY

Army Form C. 2118.

Place	Date	Hour	Summary of Events and Information	Remarks and references to Appendices
BERNAVILLE	23/6	am	Inspected all changes at Sew H.Qrs.	
			Went to see LIEUT BARTRUM. ST RAINVILLE - afterwards to Dy Depot H.Q. Details at DOMART.	
	24/6	am	Detrained 2 horses at M.M.S. reserve on relieving (1 of 132 Field 1 of 136 Fd Amb)	
		pm	Visited Sin train at MONTRELET	
	25/6	am	Evacuated 1 case of mumps from the M.M.R.	
		pm	Lectured at the ATTERG School HUMEROUIL from 2 to 4 pm	
	26/6	am	Went to MANNIERS from 8 C. 113 train new rechodged [unclear] in columns Inspected M.M.S. joint - moved to GORGES (of mud & front conveyance rates. Went with Col Quentin to CANDAS & found a site for horses moved by CANDAS. Visited Ist Holdals to inspect horses for casting & transfer).	
	27/6	pm	Had DDR & Army at LONGVILLIERS. Inspected arrivals for transfer & casting for the army in army team.	
	28/6	am	Went to Maillard District Remount	
	29/6	am	See Board Examination on Pte Stendals. 160 Hurdle as Pte Platon [unclear]	

WAR DIARY
or
INTELLIGENCE SUMMARY.

(Erase heading not required.)

Army Form C. 2118.

Place	Date	Hour	Summary of Events and Information	Remarks and references to Appendices
BERNAVILLE	29/6		Got appointment of Div. [?] & Recruiting - Endeavouring to get interview, given that he has a my [?] about standing for some, had to put him back a decision pending his official verdict practically al-[?] the meeting - Visit H.Q.S. [?] [?] shoes stated (1st 13 K.R.R.	
	30/6		Visited S.-L.F.G.E.R. [?] - now home after 172nd Bde down Ct. Col. had been returned from the land. After helping to move the Bde to that count. He was had considerable delay of x-rays by the N.T.B. Brw. R.A. [?] to Adv. D.O. Bde down at a Armouds long had condition & well cared for	
	31/6		Renton	

A.D.S. 36th Div.
Vol: 5

Army Form C. 2118.

Instructions regarding War Diaries and Intelligence Summaries are contained in F.S. Regs., Part II and the Staff Manual respectively. Title pages will be prepared in manuscript.

WAR DIARY
or
INTELLIGENCE SUMMARY.
(Erase heading not required.)

Place	Date	Hour	Summary of Events and Information	Remarks and references to Appendices
BERNAVILLE	1/6	a.m.	Visited Lieut. McLEOD 4th Bn. to see A.D.V.S. & returning arrangements in his Bde. area. Did not see him, as in spite of my wire he had had to go to SARTON to establish Remounts. Found out some particulars from his Clerk & saw the advanced collecting post. Inspected surplus horses at the M.V.S.	
	2/6	a.m.	Visited the V.S. (CANDAS) to inspect 3 horses & 1 mule which had been subjected to the intra-dermo-palpebral test on the 31st ult. & other hypodermic test yesterday. No reaction to date.	
		p.m.	Office — Submitted (clarified) indent of the Division for Remounts — Spoke with D.D.V.S. on phone re my Return of Sick & Brit. Mullein Testing, which although made out last Fred. Carr etc. did not appear to be understood by him. He called for an awarded Return. As I am floored with a doddering idiot for a Clerk, all the clerical labour falls on myself, I am working late to-night. Down later as to-ped until the days are longer — to-morrow I attended. The reserve of the M.V.S. from CANDAS not sur definitely fixed — half post of S.C. to remain Rattled & will go to DOULLENS from the 4th inst. with an advanced collecting Post. at ACHEUX. It will be a long distance to evacuate from the front.	

WAR DIARY
or
INTELLIGENCE SUMMARY.

(Erase heading not required.)

Army Form C. 2118.

Place	Date	Hour	Summary of Events and Information	Remarks and references to Appendices
BERNAVILLE	3/2/16	am	Visited M.V.S. at CANDAS to inspect 2 horses & 1 mule belonging to Div: Sig: Coy, Div: Cavalry & 122nd Field Coy R.E. These animals were retested by the intra palpebral method on the 31st ult. & hypodermically on the 1st inst. – No m/ pren dextford reactions during Dn! Testing. The Div: Cavalry horse gave a negative retest – The remaining 3 animals are still doubtful, both of them having thrown out a local reaction at the 36th hour although there was none at the 20th hour on any temp. reaction. Reported mule by wire to Dir. S.[?] Army. Case Reserve reported by O.C. Inspn & received from 1/1st Cheshire Fd. R.T.A. Reported same to S.D.V.S. Also called for report from VO 1/1st Cheshire Bde. Office – Captain Crouchie & Thorn called – Gave former instructions the moving to the new area this change over. Captain Thorn came to report re the progress of the animals retested. Reported to the D.D.V.S. that the administration of the remainder of this 53rd brchistsis[?] battling was however over by the 46th Divn from the 2nd inst – Telegraphed Divn. Re move of mules from the in-reliated animals & asked approval to destroy the mule belonging to 122nd Field Coy from – Inspected the retested animals at the M.V.S.	
BERNAVILLE	4/7/16	am		

Army Form C. 2118.

WAR DIARY
or
INTELLIGENCE SUMMARY.
(Erase heading not required.)

Instructions regarding War Diaries and Intelligence Summaries are contained in F.S. Regs., Part II. and the Staff Manual respectively. Title pages will be prepared in manuscript.

Place	Date	Hour	Summary of Events and Information	Remarks and references to Appendices
BERNAVILLE	4/16		Received wire from Command-Attching School HAVERNAS asking me of kindly believe on daily. Replied improbable as have arranged for L. to ACHEUX to see ADVS v/Div in connection with our move to 4/5 Div area. On view of Im move Am Div? have asked DDVS to be relieved of their lecturing.	
"	5/16	am	Visited ACHEUX to see ADVS w/Div - W/Sel. returned from leave - saw the acting DDVS (CAPT. BATT of Col. Venn unfit for particulars - Collected DDVS' Mare retatinising & reaction to retaining.	
"		pm	Visited Smith & delivered a mule belonging to 4/22 - field Cy, R.E. Shick had given a reaction although not defined to exrelat by the intraputposal hypodermic method - Could not so nuoscopic leave out motion - have telephoned to the Expert Cy for another doubtful reaction on relating to him a relieved for further testing. Received a wire to aroual officers note for the new suggested bronchine from Corp - arranged collector distribution.	
"	6/16	am	Orders published for the 48th hastalions to more to ACHEUX on the 9 instant.
Office Runtin - from officer - weekly Returns	

1577 Wt. W10791/1773 500,000 1/15 D. D. & L. A.D.S.S./Forms/C. 2118.

WAR DIARY
or
INTELLIGENCE SUMMARY.
(Erase heading not required.)

Army Form C. 2118.

Place	Date	Hour	Summary of Events and Information	Remarks and references to Appendices
ACHEUX	7/6	a.m.	2nd Lieut McQuaid moved from BERNAVILLE to ACHEUX. The Division has been moving into this new area for the past 3 or 4 days.	
		p.m.	Officer allotted duties of Veg. Offico. C. in C. 2 VBs left by bus & Sub Sec. Vet. Sub Artillery HS- CAPT. BATT & LIEUT ANDERSON - O base to portion of Div. horses. The 4th Div. Artillery are back near SARTON outside our Divl. area, + will be administrated by the A.D.V.S. 4th DIV.	
	8/6	a.m.	A.D.V.S. 4th Div tried a hut and arranged meeting of common interest - Spent some time trying to find a suitable place for the Div. V.S. Finally succeeded in doing so.	
		p.m.	Notified of his arrival to take of Remounts at DOULLENS tomorrow - Instructed O.C. M.V.S. re meeting & distributing, also arranged embarking parties - Applied to DDVS 3rd Army for permission to put in for leave	
	9/6	a.m.	Went to DOULLENS to meet remounts - Made down in lorry - did not remain - Inst Corpl. O.C. M.V.S. back to ACHEUX to arrange his billets.	
		p.m.	Horses received from ADVS 4th Div reporting a case of mange from 68th Bty. R.F.A. at ORVILLE. Instructed LIEUT ANDERSON to take over Vety charge of 68th Bty.	

Place	Date	Hour	Summary of Events and Information	Remarks and references to Appendices
ACHEUX	10/9/16	am	Inspected 32 Bde Amn Col at ACHEUX. Condition general & standing good. Stall arrangement good & hard free from disease. Inspected 14th Bde Amn Col at ACHEUX. Same remarks apply as above. Inspected 16th & 19th Hy Batty at ACHEUX. Animals rather crowded in their standings, but no Colic &c. satisfactory. Condition of animals good. Inspected 107th Bde Amn Col at Forceville. Found a number of horses in isolation, under treatment for skin disease. Undoubtedly suffering from mange. Ordered an evacuation of 11 animals. Reported to D.D.V.S. 3rd Army & to A.D.V.S. 11th Div. Ordered all animals to be clipped out & unusual precautions to be taken.	
"	11/9/16	am	Inspected horse standings & animals of the 9th & 10th Batts R. hrm. Fus. in ACHEUX. Also of 7th Fd. Coy. Engrs. RE. All animals on permanent standings or under cover. Arrangement satisfactory. Condition general good. Inspected animals & standing of 107th Inf Bde at FORCEVILLE. The standings of the battalions unsatisfactory & very muddy. Condition of animals expected much below good. Also inspected 121st Field Coy, R.E.	

Army Form C. 2118.

WAR DIARY
or
INTELLIGENCE SUMMARY.
(Erase heading not required.)

Place	Date	Hour	Summary of Events and Information	Remarks and references to Appendices
ACHEUX	11/76	a.m.	Annual Conference in a field with no permanent standing. Very muddy. Reported to Div. H.Q. in reserve - or making permanent standings as soon as possible. Visited MAILLY and inspected standings of the 122nd & 150th Field Coys R.E. Both permanent over foot.	
		p.m.	Office	
	12/76	a.m.	Visited a Section of No. 36 D.A.C. at BELLE EGLISE FARM and requested the D.A.D.M.G. to see the DAC. I then knew standings & report. If they were fit for occupation as the lower as permanent standings - inspected after a ? came to the conclusion that they could manage until well by changing their standings frequently & using the retailed roads in the form as standings.	
		p.m.	Visited MAILLY - AUCHONVILLERS & made a hur. Inspection of some of the trenches. Reported BDVS. 3 horses evacuated inspection home from 195th Batg 2nd Mtn Bde.	
ACHEUX	13/76	a.m.	Visited 167 Div. Bde. Trestor Gun Cos horses in MAILLY wood, and	

WAR DIARY
or
INTELLIGENCE SUMMARY

Army Form C. 2118.

Place	Date	Hour	Summary of Events and Information	Remarks and references to Appendices
ACHEUX	13/7/16	a.m.	Inspected all animals. Condition satisfactory, & on good standings. 2 mules shown up for casting, one too small, other bad worker; found Transport Officer & explained several points; he was in doubt about, as to the welfare of the horses.	
ACHEUX	14/7/16	a.m.	Visited all units billetted in the town & examined all horses & mules of Sandy. Visited No. 48 M.V.S. and consulted with O.C. Re: 1 mule cast.	
		p.m.	Attended to correspondence in office under guidance of A.D.V.S.	
	15/7/16	a.m.	Visited several Watering Areas in various units in FORCEVILLE; proceeded to examine horses of 12th R.I.R. and found them in & field on no proper standings; transport officer in trouble, so found Quartermaster & explained that conditions must be improved very soon. Proceeded to MAILLY WOOD & examined all R.E. horses there in good standings & sheltered. Proceeded to ENGELBELMER & examined ½ charge of 108th Bde Mach. Gun Coy. re casting.	
		p.m.	Office.	
ACHEUX	16/7/16	a.m.	Visited R.S. Companies at FORCEVILLE, ENGELBELMER & MAILLY WOOD	

WAR DIARY or INTELLIGENCE SUMMARY.

Army Form C. 2118.

Place	Date	Hour	Summary of Events and Information	Remarks and references to Appendices
ACHEOX	16.16	a.m.	Examined several horses which required veterinary attention	
		p.m.	Office.	
ACHEOX	17.16	a.m.	Arranged with for removals & sent to Q. to be forwarded to DDVS 3rd Army; Correspondence to various units; & spoke to them to find horses for casting for removal from "LEALVILLERS" on the 18th inst. for inspection by D.D.V.S. 3rd Army.	
		p.m.	Visited 3rd Entrenching Battalion, 230th Coy R.E. Army horse 12th R.G.R. at Forceville. had horses of last draught moved from a very muddy field into billets on dry standings; all under cover.	
ACHEOX	18.16	a.m.	Met DDVS 3rd Army at LEALVILLERS and had all horses to be cleared up for casting on parade at H.Q. 36th Div Train - 6 Cas. by DDR & Pent-chaufouver 16.48 M.V.S. for Evacuation.	
		p.m.	Office.	

Place	Date	Hour	Summary of Events and Information	Remarks and references to Appendices
ACHEUX	19/2/16	a.m.	Visited FORCEVILLE put Sgt. Hibbert & inspected Sick horses of several units at Present Gazette in that village. Sent 2 horses of 9th R.J.R. to 48 M.V.S.—	
		p.m.	Office & made out a A.F.A. 2000 for Wk. Ending 17/2/16 in order to complete list for summary & returns.	
ACHEUX	20/2/16	a.m.	Told full Dpth. Zwollen. 1 Bay horse at French Kavson, not full marked **Nasal Catarrh**.	
		p.m.	Office & read out numerous weekly returns to D.D.V.S. 3rd Army	
ACHEUX	21/2/16	a.m.	Visited FORCEVILLE & inspected Range in contact horses of 1st 157th How. Bat. Amn. Col. — had movement of those animals postponed from 23rd to 28th Feby. to permit of ample time to have all horses dressed 3 times over with Ca. Sulphide. All horns were clipped. — D.D.V.S. was informed officially by letter of this arrangement for V.D. 761. Visited other units in the town & inspected some horses of R.12.R.J.R.	
		p.m.	Office	

WAR DIARY
or
INTELLIGENCE SUMMARY.

(Erase heading not required.)

Army Form C. 2118.

Instructions regarding War Diaries and Intelligence Summaries are contained in F. S. Regs., Part II. and the Staff Manual respectively. Title pages will be prepared in manuscript.

Place	Date	Hour	Summary of Events and Information	Remarks and references to Appendices
ACHEUX	22/6	a.m.	Visited FORCEVILLE – horses of 127 How. Bde. Amm. Col. – Inspection all sick horses in vicinity from Units in my Bdy. Charge – proceeded to ENGELBELMER, and looked at chargers & other horses requiring vety. attention.	
		p.m.	Office.	
ACHEUX	23/6	a.m.	Visited FORCEVILLE both Capt. Crown – horses of 127 How. Bde. Amm. Col. all being prepared for the recent time path 2nd Colo. Inspt. Soln. – visited horses of 230 R. Coy R.S. Army troops & horses of D.A.R.O.R. The former in the process of making dry pluggings of chalk & cinders. the latter already on good hard brick standings.	
		p.m.	Office.	
ACHEUX	24/6	a.m.	Visited MAILLY Wood. – Evacuated 2 chargers from H.Q. 109 Lay. Bde. Suspected mange. One horse ordinarily covered with hairs & very itchy. the other, not so, but also very itchy. – Received horse from D.A.R. 3rd Army. about arrival of 54 remounts to 36th D.V. in conjunction with Capt. Greene, made
		p.m.	Went to 36th D.V.	

Army Form C. 2118.

WAR DIARY
or
INTELLIGENCE SUMMARY.
(Erase heading not required.)

Place	Date	Hour	Summary of Events and Information	Remarks and references to Appendices
ACHEUX	24/7/16	p.m.	Necessary arrangements by telegram for conducting parties to meet removals at DOULLENS Stn. on the 26th inst.	
ACHEUX	25/7/16	a.m.	Visited Sick horses of 36th Div. H.Q. - met Sgt. Abbott A.V.C. and arranged return for various units of 107th Inf. Bde.	
		p.m.	Office - ? made out A.F.A. 2000/a for various units in Vet.y charge. Sent off telegram to C.R.A. 36th Div. Arty. re time of arrival of removals, place + date.	
	26/7/16		} Routine	
	27/7/16			
	28/7/16	a.m.	Inspected Prob Vet: Lie — Inspected the 127th Mons/Bde Ammn Col at FORCEVILLE in relation to mange outbreak. All animals of this unit are now clipped as they have been known 3 times with Ca. Biniodyd. Solution — CAPT. CHOWN in Vet.y charge has carried out and all details of disinfection + prevention org. Strongly. Visited lines of 230th Army 2nd yn Coy R.E. & 121st Field Coy. R.E. latter have not yet completed their permanent standings. Reported my return from leave by wire to D.D.V.S.	

Army Form C. 2118.

WAR DIARY
or
INTELLIGENCE SUMMARY.
(Erase heading not required.)

Place	Date	Hour	Summary of Events and Information	Remarks and references to Appendices
ACHEUX	27/16	pm	Office - held return &c.	
	28/16	am	Inspected 2 animals at the 74 VS. selected for the second time yesterday by the veterinary pathol. & noted - horse catarrh. Inspected the 172 Bde Amm Col. which has just arrived in ACHEUX - animals looking very well - are on pace hard standings.	
		pm	Inspected the 46 Fd Amm Col at ARQUEVES - shoe dubbins ny - arrived all in stable - outside very pood, feeding & watering arrangements & general stable management very pood - 173 Bde RFA arrived in ACHEUX from the training area.	
	29/16	am	Went round with Captn D Connachie to inspect the standings of horses under his charge at ENGLEBELMER & MAILLY -	
		pm	Office.	

ADVS
36rd
Vol 6

Place	Date	Hour	Summary of Events and Information	Remarks and references to Appendices
ACHEUX	1/3/16	am.	Went to ORVILLE to meet the A.D.V.S. 4th Div to discuss mange outbreak in a batty at that place. With a view to the possibility of this Div'n taking over ORVILLE. Also observed the mange outbreak in the 127th Bde Ammn Col (4th Div) at present in ACHEUX & the measures taken to control same. As one of this batt's brigades came from ACHEUX, arranged with A.D.V.S. 4th Div from vet on to inspect sick on tomorrow, in order that we might decide as to removing restrictions etc. Home from A.D.V.S. 3rd Army asking for the return of the strength of all Units in horses & mules by classes. Had already written him regretting that it was impossible to furnish an accurate return in the weekly returns just submitted owing to the shortness of the notice received, & Units being actively employed & on the move. Have wired to Vet Lt/Sergt. An Tsures Lt. La Return cannot be anything but most inaccurate & approximate. Inspected the standings of the 172nd & 173rd Bdes R.F.A. in ACHEUX wood. Have marked a strong report to G.H.Q. regarding the state of these places, being a sea of liquid manure. Hardstands could be found, but Men to feed sufficiently. Finding Steam Whipe kept most of the animals	

Army Form C. 2118.

WAR DIARY
or
INTELLIGENCE SUMMARY.
(Erase heading not required.)

Instructions regarding War Diaries and Intelligence Summaries are contained in F.S. Regs., Part II. and the Staff Manual respectively. Title pages will be prepared in manuscript.

Place	Date	Hour	Summary of Events and Information	Remarks and references to Appendices
ACHEUX	1. 3/16	p.m.	arrived out of the wood within the next day or two. Officer in that town there will be great trouble from Sanguineous dermatitis etc. This Brigade from today is in 4th Army (10th Corps).	
"	2. 3/16	a.m.	Inspected 127th How Bde Ammn Col with ADVS. 4th Div. He was very satisfied with the condition of the animals. He received however 3 horses three of whom had been a little flushed with the dressing, as it was difficult to tie over. Rest they were clean. Other Commanders very acutely. Visited the 154th, 156th R.F.a. at LOUVENCOURT and inspected the horses and Camp. Condition of animals fair — Lines in a field with no permanent standings consequently much —	
"	3. 3/16	p.m.	Office — Received Divisional weekly indent for Remounts.	
"	"	p.m.	Visited several units in ACHEUX to inspect new sites of standings. Called at 111.25 Art. Train at LEAVILLERS. Saw the O.C. Damaged Inspect. his animals tomorrow — Rode round to inspect the standings of the Corps — All horses in Good permanent standings.	
"	"	p.m.	Office. Spoke with DDVS 5th Army on phone. Submitted report on 3 horses evacuated	

Army Form C. 2118.

WAR DIARY
or
INTELLIGENCE SUMMARY.
(Erase heading not required.)

Instructions regarding War Diaries and Intelligence Summaries are contained in F. S. Regs., Part II. and the Staff Manual respectively. Title pages will be prepared in manuscript.

Place	Date	Hour	Summary of Events and Information	Remarks and references to Appendices
MOLLIENS	3/3/16	p.m.	expected yesterday from 177th Hvy Bde Amm Col. with unexpected orange.	
"	4/3/16	a.m.	Started to go to PERNOIS in a car to visit 153 Bde RG but needed to work. Co had moving hard. Took O.C. M.V.S. to DOULLENS to entrain sick horses. Had arranged to inspect 36-5 Sect from at LEALVILLERS, but got held up on road from DOULLENS to LEALVILLERS & was unable to keep appointment.	
		p.m.	Office – Forwarded Wfs of correspondence re Course of Farriery BDDVS & Army. Worked DDVS & Army Sobbing Factories Mobile sick horses from 153rd Bde at PERNOIS might be evacuated – also re appointment of an A.V.C. Sgt. to 76th Hy Batty to replace one awaiting trial by Court Martial. BDVS & Army & DDR & Army called at HQ and also talked over routine matters. BDVS inspected the 48th Mob Vet Sec.	
	5/3/16	a.m.	from Visited BERTRANCOURT to look around & see twentieth accompanied for horses – saw the O.C. 6.5 Sqd. Army Dragoons. Inspected one of his horses & recent Remount for detritits – Unable to send Mf weekly ammung returns as no returns been received from V.O. 153rd Bde RJA at PERNOIS	

Army Form C. 2118.

WAR DIARY
or
INTELLIGENCE SUMMARY.
(Erase heading not required.)

Instructions regarding War Diaries and Intelligence Summaries are contained in F.S. Regs., Part II. and the Staff Manual respectively. Title pages will be prepared in manuscript.

Place	Date	Hour	Summary of Events and Information	Remarks and references to Appendices
ACHEUX	6/3/16	a.m.	Office - weekly returns - Inspected the 36th Div! train at LEALVILLERS - General state Vet. room - Condition General Good, sheep satisfactory, General state & management - Good. All companies are in brick standings which, although there are very good and the accommodation is ample. Arrived for 12 men to be attached to the Sub. Vet. See from the Div! Res. Train in making horse standings.	
	7/3/16	a.m.	Inspected 108 Field Ambulance at FORCEVILLE - Recent stopgaps, but had to call attention to broken agent washing horses. Inspected 107/54 BAC. & then rode on - Visited ENGLEBELMER & rode on destination to those belonging to 122 Field Coy R.E. Sufferers from white lice. Arranged for MARTINSART to see his accommodation in hours of the 109 Heavy Bde just moved in -	
		p.m.	Office - Capt. McCLINTOCK (P.O. 173rd Brigade) & LIEUT PAUL (No. 153 F.C.R.S.) Came to see me. Inspected horses in M.V.S. both evacuated Unknowns. Set a supplementary return for Remounts. Reported D.D.V.S. one storage wounded from 153rd Bde R.F.A.	

Army Form C. 2118.

WAR DIARY
or
INTELLIGENCE SUMMARY.
(Erase heading not required.)

Instructions regarding War Diaries and Intelligence Summaries are contained in F. S. Regs., Part II. and the Staff Manual respectively. Title pages will be prepared in manuscript.

Place	Date	Hour	Summary of Events and Information	Remarks and references to Appendices
ACHEUX	8/3/16	a.m.	Inspected the 153rd Bde R.F.A. — Condition of horses on the whole not unsatisfactory — showing not up to mark. This Bde has experienced great difficulty in getting a sufficient number of shoes whilst away from their Division. Found 6 horses in a Battery in A Battery suffering from their shoes — having cracked hoofs, fears of contraction. Had these removed, also in one cases Corns. Take large because shoes due to this. Left these too slow in some cases. Condition of the horses around the food of scarcely satisfactory. Gave them one suggested. Dressings followed all 6 to be executed. 159 Bot horses by some destroyed. 110 6 Bde Horses clipped out and examined with Col. Biney & Col. Hlake this morning. Precautions with regard to contamination. The interior being placed in working solution. Reported extraction of a case of suspected mange from the 19th Hy Batty gunr BOT.	
		p.m.	Visited BERTANCOURT BEAUSSART & MAILY — Inspected the 50th Field Cy at MAILY. Horses looking very well & are in an excellent standing — Gave a circular to all V.Os. calling attention to the Report of the finding	

1577 Wt. W10791/1773 500,000 1/15 D. D. & L. A.D.S.S./Forms/C. 2118.

WAR DIARY or INTELLIGENCE SUMMARY

Army Form C. 2118.

Place	Date	Hour	Summary of Events and Information	Remarks and references to Appendices
ACHEUX	8/7/16		Issuing of dead labels in order purchase information - asked for a reply of all dead certificates with a record of post-mortem examinations.	
"	9/7/16	a.m.	Inspected the Rest Camp at VARENNES — It is turning out to be so pairs of shoes per diem & moving chiefly to the Artillery. Visited HEDAUVILLE & inspected the transport-lines of the 12th & 13th R.I. Rifles. The 12th R.I.R. have good transport lines & bindings & the animals were looking very fit & well cared for. Saw 2 horse recently clipped that showed evidence of severe infection with lice. Also I think these horses are badly distressed from using too Clumsy a disinfectant, & unable to looking wet. Told the transport officer that washing must only be done under Veterinary orders. The 13th R.I.R. transport lines looking very well cared for. All under cover. Shells horses etc.	
"		p.m.	Office — Wrote Asst. Dir. Vet. Service Dept. for further information.	
"	10/7/16	a.m.	Inspected 173rd Brigade R.F.A. — R.A.C. at ACHEUX, battery lines in ENGELBELMER wood. Condition of horses of the Am. Col. not satisfactory. Attributed this to the	

WAR DIARY
or
INTELLIGENCE SUMMARY.

Place	Date	Hour	Summary of Events and Information	Remarks and references to Appendices
ACHEUX	10/7/16	a.m.	The entire unit Hy have recently been very (b) adverse condition under which they existed in ACHEUX Wood for the first week of their arrival here (c) the scarcity of sand eaten at their training camp, where they have large numbers of cuis of sand colic. The condition of the baggage horses was satisfactory, but they as surrounded in the standings at ENGLEBELMER or the surroundings. The standings are appalling being knee deep in mud though did the horse have been several times daily. Submitted report to S.V.2 recommending that the hay ration of the Rile kerbel be made up to 12lbs and for the next month. also that as few animals as possible be kept in ENGLEBELMER Wood.	
		p.m.	Officer - Drafted Remount Indention for Ant Order.	
	11/7/16	a.m.	Inspected some horses in M.V.S. evacuated from 36 S.A.C. for debility. They were by means debilitated & should not have been evacuated. Instructed O.C. M.V.S. to return them to their unit & write M.D.O. on the subject. Inspected the 194th Field Coy. R.E. with new breaking ring horses. Found 7 of 5 H.D. to be changed for L.D. - 20 horses cheaped by the Unit as H.D. are not	

Army Form C. 2118.

WAR DIARY
or
INTELLIGENCE SUMMARY.
(Erase heading not required.)

Place	Date	Hour	Summary of Events and Information	Remarks and references to Appendices
ACHEUX	11/7/16	a.m.	H.D. & should not have been on Chiefield.	
		p.m.	Office - Received wire re arrival of Remounts at DOULLENS at 6 am on 12th inst. Reported to OPPS R.A. that my instructions re horses in 153rd Bde R.A. were not being carried out & asking that effect should be given to them immediately. Received instructions from OSVS 4th Army re Academy Board of 2nd Lieut A Chitty	
	12/7/16	a.m.	To Le Tourne Croise at ABBEVILLE	
		p.m.	Office - Weekly Returns	
	13/7/16	a.m.	Inspected mules arrived Remounts at Mob. Vet. Sec. Visited BERTRANCOURT. Went with DAQMG to inspect "An ISD" & 122nd Field Corps R.E. at MAILLY with a view to classifying the horses. In 122nd Coy classified only 6 as H.D - These units have been drawing 8 - In 150 Coy classified 10 as H.D - This unit has been drawing 16 - All these H.D. are maintained, will be transferred in due course by order of DDR 4th Army.	
		p.m.	Visited MAILY & ENGLEBELMER to see where units were located. Placed Lieut MILLER in [?] charge of 2 Bells 172 Bde - Appointed Capt. Charon as Vet. Inspector ACHEUX to deal with disease in animals of [?] undoubtedly	

WAR DIARY or INTELLIGENCE SUMMARY

Army Form C. 2118.

Place	Date	Hour	Summary of Events and Information	Remarks and references to Appendices
ACHEUX	13/6	1 pm	Forwarded & recommended a suggestion from the C.R.A. that a course of instruction in hot shoeing should be inaugurated. He does not wish to send any men for a course in cold shoeing.	
"	14/6	3 am	Inspected all Artillery lines in BERTRANCOURT & BEAUSSART viz 2 Batt? 154" Bde, 1 Batt? 172" Bde and a section of B.A.C. All animals under cover in barns, sheds etc. Condition on the whole quite satisfactory. Shoeing fair. Water supply in BERTRANCOURT a large pond from which water is pumped into troughs – should not give out – in BEAUSSART a small pond which will not last through the summer – supply elsewhere ample. Hay seems to be fair. Common forms, ladders around stables & stafftrees. Inspected lines for evacuation of sick at the Turf Vet. Sec. Also arranged for disposal of outflow remounts. Reported arrival of 1 Sgt, J. Davies at 19 Hy Batt. & 36 Oth Lieut Cpt at ARQUEVES & BELLE EGLISE FME. Inspected all animals. Made my last inspection. Since my last inspection there is still room for more improvement in this section. Too many poor beasts in this section.	
"	15/6	6 am		

1577 Wt. W10791/1773 500,000 1/15 D. D. & L. A.D.S.S./Forms/C. 2118.

WAR DIARY
or
INTELLIGENCE SUMMARY.
(Erase heading not required.)

Army Form C. 2118.

Place	Date	Hour	Summary of Events and Information	Remarks and references to Appendices
ACHEUX	15/7/16	a.m.	and enough attention does not appear to be paid to the past. The harness of horses & their grooming could also do to be good — horses are not losing their fat — but the 3 Echos well looked after — The stamp of mule is W.S.R. is not good on the whole — they are an unknown Qty, with a large percentage of untrained deffs, field side animals, difficult trips in evolution. Submitted an Inspection report to D.D.V.S. Wrote report wildly calling attention to the mules in her gazette. Capt Chavers invited such should be at once R.C. to Routine. Received Proceedings of Court Martial on Sergeant Jones 45th M.V.S. who was charged with being drunk in POSSEUILLE — believe of Court "to reduce to Corporal". Issued first copy of Routine Order by myself to all R.Os. — Appointed Cook V.O. & Veg. Inspector of certain villages to deal with contagious disease among animals. Inhabitants take to readin assistance when necessary.	
	16/7/16	a.m.	Routine - office. Submitted to Amglop Ident for Removals for Bonnen	

Place	Date	Hour	Summary of Events and Information	Remarks and references to Appendices
ACHEUX	16/6	p.m.	Inspected mm horses of 173 Bde R.F.A. and 6 Bde H.D. — Some of the horses could be dangerous or H.D. Visited MARTINSART & MESNIL. X Batty R.H.A. & 135th Army Troops Coy R.E. arrived in this Dist. area today — arranged vety attendance. to affect their new troop WO re stating that part of remounts being Charges. They executing other than those of the owners in accordance with instructions from S.D.V.S. 4th Army.	
	17/6	a.m.	Routine	
		p.m.	Visited SARTON to inspect the Camps of 1, 3 Bde Ammn Cols lately formed there — Each lines two brick standings & canvas shelters between, the horses are kept out in open fields during the day, which is a good plan. The surroundings & latrines are not very sanitary, as the unit in recent occupation have been in the habit of throwing up the manure around the stables, which will be a great breeding ground for flies later on — Submitted a report to the Div. asking the several S.Hb. minor is own to provide. forwarded an application for lamps of Approved Pattern 48th V.S. 6 S.D.V.S. 4 Army.	

Army Form C. 2118.

WAR DIARY or INTELLIGENCE SUMMARY.

Place	Date	Hour	Summary of Events and Information	Remarks and references to Appendices
ACHEUX	18/3	a.m.	Visited ORVILLE transport lines & "B" Bty R.H.A. & "X" Batty R.H.A. lines having just arrived & been attached to this Bde for administration. The 15-4" B.A.C. are in good order standing with canvas shelters. The horses in fair condition but there is a good deal of laminitis which is almost unavoidable with the heavy work they are carrying. The hovey cart not up to date. "X" Batty also in good standing. All the horses of this Batty are clipped out and in excellent condition. It was a great pleasure to inspect a unit so well looked after. Horses thoroughly well groomed. One could not but appreciate the difference — the management between the 2nd Army & the 4th, although it is unfair to tell the same standard for both.	
		p.m.	Rode Ruitin[?] Walker around various units in ACHEUX. Officer weekly returns.	
	19/10	3 am to 10 am	Visited MARTINSART & inspected the horse standing of 109 Bde Mn G Coy & the 9th & 10 R. Innis. Fus. The M.G. Coy are such an unhappy rabble as ever.	

WAR DIARY or INTELLIGENCE SUMMARY

Army Form C. 2118.

Place	Date	Hour	Summary of Events and Information	Remarks and references to Appendices
ACHEUX	19/3/16	p.m.	The armn. at 9 pm, 9.10 pm. Abram Inn are detached about in Acheux. There are too many animals in MARTINSART which can be put under shelter. Besides 3 hy. Batt. Draught lines there are Reserve Pack Horses and a field coy. R.E. Personally undesirably splitting into lines into huts, but informed that it is impossible for the present.	
	20/3/16	a.m.	Inspected "A" Batty 153 Bde R.F.A. This Batty had several horses evacuated. Inspected range. The cupping this infection from which the Corn were evacuated is not yet completed – several additional animals fair – lice every prevalent. Also inspected Draught lines of 14 S.R.J.R. in HEDAUVILLE – horses were in huts, well looked after – in the open – both managed – outpickets – Condition of Riding food, but H.D. poor. The latter are in the worst part of a food stamp. V.O. reports present shortage of hay rations:	
		p.m.	Inspected armn. of 109" Field Ambulance – Condition very good, animals of a coot dairy well looked after. – Reported inspected lines. Horses from 8th R.J.R. R.D.O.V.S. 4th Army.	

1577 Wt. W10791/1773 500,000 1/15 D. D. & L. A.D.S.S./Forms/C. 2118.

Place	Date	Hour	Summary of Events and Information	Remarks and references to Appendices
ACHEUX	20/7/16	pm	Sanctioned leave for Capt. CHOWN O.C. 48th Mob. Vet. Sec. from 23 inst. and rearranged duties.	
	21/7/16	am	Inspected A. & B. sub.Sys. 172 Bde - condition of horses fair - there were present - but much time on the way of grooming as there are very few men for the purpose - Inspected animals of 3rd Monmouth. Regt. at FORCEVILLE - found fault with several practices in looking horses, generally declining - horses had sadly neglected appearance. Received notification from A.D.V.S. 49th Divn that he was estimating this Unit - Replied that I was inspecting the Veterinary arrangements in the 36th Divisional area - Called at the office of 150 Field Coy & spoke re the spreading of manure at present it is piled in heaps of a long banks immediately behind the standings.	
		pm	Office - both D.D.V.S. & Adm re Vet Activities - two out areas forwarded to Director from Corps activities - Inspected sick cases in 2nd B Vet Sec.	
	22/7/16	am	DDVS & Adm called to Corps on arrange re the 53 Bde R.F.A.	
		pm	Visited MARTINSART R/Cy of Front & Sec for the horses at present in the	

WAR DIARY
or
INTELLIGENCE SUMMARY.
(Erase heading not required.)

Army Form C. 2118.

Place	Date	Hour	Summary of Events and Information	Remarks and references to Appendices
ACHEUX	22/6	pm	In the relieve of MARTINSART. Read Plan with Cmdr. in MARTINSART wood but it was muddy at present. Shall advise putting all horses etc in about fortnight's time. Received wire re arrival of Remount trimmers, & made the necessary arrangements. Photos. re wiring re for two wagons of forage (Morphia) in have evacuated from 51st R.J.R. & 2nd batty 153rd Bde RFA — Reptd to RTO. Visited by Received wire to attend conference at office of sorts 4th Army at 3pm tomorrow.	
	23/6	am	Rept to Corps Commander at Railhead. BOR with my war personal.	
		pm	Attended a conference at offices of sorts 4th Army.	
	24/6	am	Routine.	
		pm	Inspected Bird. Horse at WARENNES, also arrival of 15th R.J.R. at FORCEVILLE. Received orders to send Pte Richards MC. via Abbeville & see to Inglund. He having been accepted as a cadet for a commission.	
	25/6	am	Visited LEALVILLERS to see the forge & M. Burgain & speak re for particularly of obtaining a shoeing smith. Course due. Went on to RAINCHEVAL.	

WAR DIARY
or
INTELLIGENCE SUMMARY.
(Erase heading not required.)

Army Form C. 2118.

Place	Date	Hour	Summary of Events and Information	Remarks and references to Appendices
ACHEUX	25/3/16	am	RAINCHEVAL and inspected the animals of the 16th R.I.R (Rovers) — Condition satisfactory. Mainly "Phthisis" in bad condition — evacuated a H.D. horse into chronic freema.	
		pm	Received useful inspection of all animals of "A" Batty 153" Bde at HÉDAUVILLE. This Batty has had several been Mange. Horses on suspicious care in isolation — evacuated same. Remainder of animals looking well although his are prevalent— urged on Vet Officer, and of all horses & arranged to land clipping machines. The V.O. to this Bn finished inspection of this morning & had me to see the horses he had isolated. One catarrhic with some chronic of lachymia chuck appeared other then very well formed lattis.	
	26/3/16	am	Off. is weekly returns —	
		pm	Visited HARPONVILLE & VARENNES with the Object of selecting a suitable site for the new Vet. See as he shall shortly be evacuating ACHEUX — Went to these & spoke much helpee — Received orders to transfer Opl Frane 48" M.V.S. to No 3 Vet Hospital.	

WAR DIARY
or
INTELLIGENCE SUMMARY.
(Erase heading not required.)

Army Form C. 2118.

Place	Date	Hour	Summary of Events and Information	Remarks and references to Appendices
ACHEUX	27/3/16	am	Routine – Inspected S.A.A. Lee of 173. B.A.C. in ACHEUX. The condition of the horses of this B.A.C. was reported on badly by me about 3 weeks ago. S.A.A. section now looking very well – Propose inspecting the remainder of this B.A.C. at SARTON next Wednesday. Arranged with Q. to start a short farrier course of 6 weeks to instruct at GHQ No 945 (in attestations of untrained men) starting with 6 candidates selected in places – 1 per Infantry Bde – 1 per Field Coy R.E. The letter will get the allotments for the ABBEVILLE Course. Gave instruction for a horse of S. Batty 172 Bde suffering from septic arthritis a sequel of suppurous dermatitis.	
		pm	Inspected 36th Fd. Cavalry at BERTRANCOURT – Horse lately rec'd, but numbers could be fed: Ries bellies will average – Meeing good. Full complement of during smiths & 2 spare just returned from the Course at ABBEVILLE. Markings good and very even spread – antiseptics – Gun Division moves to CONTAY tomorrow.	
	28/3/16	am	Met Lieut MUIR AVC at MAILLY and inspected Coms advanced horse lines	

WAR DIARY or INTELLIGENCE SUMMARY

Army Form C. 2118.

Place	Date	Hour	Summary of Events and Information	Remarks and references to Appendices
ACHEUX	28/3	am	Cinies. Called at Hd Quarters & saw O.C. 154th Bde R.A. Mentioned that the horses were kept to a little neglected whilst the guns were in action, as own batteries have no officer superintending the horse lines. from office - met D.D.R. & Army - Shewed him a charger which had come up with the last batch of Remounts - hopeless, & got a bridle on - the horse to be examined. Visited Bn Horse at VARIENNES & spoke with the Staff Sergt Farrier & there with reference to the horses commencing the 4th April.	
	29/3/16	am	Inspected 173 B.A.C. at SARTON to see what progress had been made since my advice report of Jan 10: inst - Found a remarkable all round improvement. Advised a report to H.Q.R.A. Also inspected Nos 153, 154 & 172" Bde Amn Cols at SARTON & ORVILLE - Horses all comfortably housed and standings clean. Improvement going on throft - Condition of all quite satisfactory. Called to see O.C. of E Batty R.H.A.	
		pm	Visited HARPONVILLE & took the Senior N.C.O. of the 48 D.M.V.S over the new billets - suit- for the trouble.	

Army Form C. 2118.

WAR DIARY
or
INTELLIGENCE SUMMARY.
(Erase heading not required.)

Instructions regarding War Diaries and Intelligence Summaries are contained in F. S. Regs., Part II. and the Staff Manual respectively. Title pages will be prepared in manuscript.

Place	Date	Hour	Summary of Events and Information	Remarks and references to Appendices
ACHEUX	30/3/16	a.m.	Visited Div: Farm & see his O.C. & arrange re a farriers course. Also & see the working of his Petrol Forge. Found that they were not having the Forge as intended — had it sent of the M.V.S. for trial. O.C. Sn: 19 in complained of the V.O. not visiting his unit every day. Rang up V.O. & gave him definite orders on the subject.	
		p.m.	Visited D Batty 172: Bde & see him working & his other Petrol Forge. Arranged for the Division for trial. Found it not being used as intended. Showed the Farrier Sn: how to use it. No intention on exercise in that any Shoes Forge had been received in Unit. & found that they had been received some time ago but no instructions as to their use. Invited to the Farrier Sn: how same were comed with them. He tried & sent to the Farm for relations. Received a Confidential letter from O.C. 36 F.A.C. complaining that his V.O. did not carry out his duties as to evidence to himself. Am going into his system. Submitted fortnightly return (confidential) for the Division — Poor Stamp of Field ambulances. A.D.S.S./Forms/C. 2118.
	31/3/16	a.m.	Inspected 118 Field Ambulance — Poor stamp of N.C.O. horse & a horse of protection

Army Form C. 2118.

WAR DIARY
or
INTELLIGENCE SUMMARY.
(Erase heading not required.)

Instructions regarding War Diaries and Intelligence Summaries are contained in F. S. Regs., Part II. and the Staff Manual respectively. Title pages will be prepared in manuscript.

Place	Date	Hour	Summary of Events and Information	Remarks and references to Appendices
ACHEUX	31/10	a.m.	Inspection of old animals — Condition very good, Stable management satisfactory — Form Office — Submitted report on forage called for by Q — Spoke to O.C. SMAV A.V.C. re complaint received from O.C. 36th D.A.C.	

Ed. Webb
Major AVC
Comdt. 36th Divn.

1577 Wt. W10791/1773 500,000 1/15 D. D. & L. A.D.S.S./Forms/C. 2118.

ADVS 36
DW
Vol 7

Army Form C. 2118.

WAR DIARY
or
INTELLIGENCE SUMMARY.
(Erase heading not required.)

Place	Date	Hour	Summary of Events and Information	Remarks and references to Appendices
ACHEUX	1/6	am	O.C. & 8th M.V.S. reported his arrival from leave. Inspected transport animals of 9th R.F. and 11th R.F.R. at Hedauville. Inspected 4 sick 153rd Bde R.F.A. — no further cases of mange during the past week.	
		pm	Took O.C. M.V.S. to Harponville & thence to Authieville — for the Mobile Section that moves on the 3rd inst. Spoke to Lt Miller re slackness in submission of weekly returns. Telegraphed weekly summary.	
	2/6	am	Routine — submitted weekly returns — Issued Routine Orders containing readjustment of duties.	
		pm	Visited Martinsart & looked round lines.	
HARPONVILLE	3/6	am	Visited 2nd to march from Acheux to Harponville. Visited Martinsart & Authieville — visited an advanced collecting post. Will need to select a suitable site for an advanced collecting post between the two.	
		pm	Held a Conference of Vet Officers & discussed measures to be taken to be formulated for put into practice during an offensive.	
	4/6	am	Inspected the 172nd Bde R.F.A. in their new Camp at Toutencourt. Pervaded O.C. before its inspection, also informed him that he considered the horses	

WAR DIARY
or
INTELLIGENCE SUMMARY
(Erase heading not required.)

Army Form C. 2118.

Place	Date	Hour	Summary of Events and Information	Remarks and references to Appendices
HARPONVILLE	4/10	a.m.	Battery is in a particularly bad way — Whilst his brigade have been in action the officers have been very bad off the horses, which have suffered but own condition, due to constant standing or bad standing on their arrival in ACHEUX, but their condition at present time is not bad, or each a the spring weather should cause considerable improvement. There is a great drawback to their present location in that they have to go 2 to 3 miles (for water).	
"		p.m.	Visited Bn. Dmps at VARENNES & opthe colt and mare of the Junior Course which commenced today — Also visited LEAVIEURS (Lieut Gard). Inspected new billet arrangements of the Gnds. Vet. See. in HARPONVILLE.	
"	5/10	a.m.	Inspected "C" Batty 73rd A.Bde. At request of O.C. Horses have fallen away considerably, due in large measure to want of supervision whilst the teams were in action — Examined several horses for ability, & carries no feeling etc. Sound exceptionally horsey — Inspected "A" Batty 73rd Bde in ENGLEBEIMER WOOD — Great improvement — "B" C Batty	
"		p.m.	Visited MARTINSART — HAMEL & AUTHUILLE	

Army Form C. 2118.

WAR DIARY
or
INTELLIGENCE SUMMARY.
(Erase heading not required.)

Instructions regarding War Diaries and Intelligence Summaries are contained in F. S. Regs., Part II. and the Staff Manual respectively. Title pages will be prepared in manuscript.

Place	Date	Hour	Summary of Events and Information	Remarks and references to Appendices
HARPONVILLE	6/4	a.m.	Routine - office	
		p.m.	Visited Pct Forge at VARENNES, saw CAPT CONNOCHIE AVC & gave him instructions re delivering to the Junior Class at present assembled. Spoke with DDVS 4th Army on the Phone - Received instructions re lecture at the Artillery School. Saw the Army in Safe road - told DDR 4th Army & asked him to arrange a day & time & place for lecting.	
	7/4	a.m.	Visited PUCHVILLERS - find MO's 36 Stat.C - inspected sick lines & horses for casting. Spoke with O.C. 36 St.C. with reference to the Complaint about the VO.	
		p.m.	Routine - office	
	8/4	a.m.	Visited A.D.V.S. 29th Divt at ACHEUX & re arrange Vet charge of certain units. Rcvd. D.D.V.S. 4th Army at his office.	
		p.m.	Lectured at the Artillery School MAYERNAS	
	9/4	a.m.	Routine - office - Inspected heads of telegraphic armoury.	
		p.m.	Visited VARENNES & FORCEVILLE - Sorted around horse camps etc.	
	10/4	a.m.	Inspected HD horse Wittomm from 150 RE Co for mine bd Svy Arm - Had the appearance of being overworked - Spoke to LtSHAW AVC re	

WAR DIARY
or
INTELLIGENCE SUMMARY.
(Erase heading not required.)

Army Form C. 2118.

Place	Date	Hour	Summary of Events and Information	Remarks and references to Appendices
HARPONVILLE	10/16	a.m.	re Blackburn Generally — Spoke to Baehnsio 36" Div Arty re new condition of Artillery horses generally & re arrangements for exchanging when the Bdes are in action — DDR Fourth Army came to inspect horses for casting for remount Reserve.	
		p.m.	Inspected B C & D Battys 154 How Bde d/ FORCEVILLE — Horses looking in better condition than the other brigades. They are very short of men & officers & took after over & large fatigues for the shipping gun pits etc.	
	11/16	a.m.	Visited HEDAUVILLE to inspect arrangements for water supply — Found them unsatisfactory & submitted report with suggestions to Q — Called at HQ 25 Div 9" Hy Bde just arrived in the area — also inspected 24 Sty Batty of Same Bde — Horses in excellent condition & a Remt. Camp.	
		p.m.	Office — Interviewed CAPT. HAYTER ho VB 9" Hy Bde — Reported arrival of this Bde with its 90 to 90 H.P. Fourth Army.	
	12/16	a.m.	Inspected 108" Hy Batty at FORCEVILLE — Condition of animals very good. Saw C Batty 153" How (slung out trench) — Shocked by their condition	

WAR DIARY or INTELLIGENCE SUMMARY

Army Form C. 2118.

Place	Date	Hour	Summary of Events and Information	Remarks and references to Appendices
HARPONVILLE	12/76	9 am	Arranged with SM2 R.E. Inspect Line Tally Tramway	
		pm	Office – hack out potentially evidence [?] no Remounts – Inspected Tr[?] Arms horses in Mr V.S. & arranges for them issue.	
	13/76	am	Inspected C Batty 153 Bde R.F.A. – Arrival in Thorley condition – looking absolutely starved neglected – Evacuated 16 Ment sick – Cases – Submitted a strong report to D ung as to state of affairs existing. Inspected 122 Ly Batty & F[?]. 29° Bde to settle a matter of Vety administration. Called on A.D.V.S. 29° Bde to settle a matter of Vety administration.	
			Office – Called at H.Q. Div Arty Brigade re C/153 Bde	
	14/76	am	Inspected all Charges in SM2 – Also D/173 Bde – Evacuated 4 horses to debility in latter – remainder of horses in good condition. The Sect Commander inspected.	
		4 pm	Visited MARTINSART & inspected the 151st & 150th Fd Coys R.E. Condition General satisfactory.	
	15/76	am	St. J.V.S. Ponsonby came to see me with reference to my application for transfer of Lieut G.K. Shaw – He also inspected the Mr.V.S. & talked over several matters.	

WAR DIARY or INTELLIGENCE SUMMARY

Army Form C. 2118.

Place	Date	Hour	Summary of Events and Information	Remarks and references to Appendices
HARPONVILLE	15/6	a.m.	matters including the question of my duties report on C/153 Bde.	
		p.m.	Inspected 154th B.A.C. at FORCEVILLE – Orders & horses to be evacuated for debility – Condition of animals as a whole fair only – The horses which have been recently clipped out on account of lice are feeling the change of weather. Also inspected B Batt 173 Bde at ACHEUX – Condition of animals quite satisfactory. Comparatively few poor ones.	
	16/6	a.m.	Inspected 182 "B" Bty R.F.A. – Condition 1 animal at fair – Evacuated 2 for debility – Inspected 12th & 13th Batt R.J.R. – Condition general 1 with battalions very satisfactory.	
		p.m.	Office.	
	17/6	a.m.	Inspected 172nd Bde R.F.A. on D Batt. – Great improvement in condition since last inspection a fortnight ago – Submitted an inspection report to H.Q. 8th Div.	
		p.m.	Inspected horses for evacuation in A.V.S. – Visited Sh/Farrier Sgt. Lowrie at VARENNES & hatched with Shu Farriers Class – Candidates making good progress	
	18/6	a.m.	Visited MEDAVILLE with D.A.Q.M.G. to inspect watering arrangements (or watering)	

WAR DIARY or INTELLIGENCE SUMMARY

Army Form C. 2118.

Place	Date	Hour	Summary of Events and Information	Remarks and references to Appendices
HAPPENVILLE	18/10	a.m.	D.D.V.S. rang up on phone to tell me to lecture at Artillery School HAVERNAS re Thurs: next.	
	19/10	a.m.	Routine office.	
		p.m.	Visited MARTINSART - met 10 & 11 R.H.A. Infantry Bdes - Inspected 9" 10" & 11" R Horses Fns. & 109" MG Coy - Condition & animals of these units quite satisfactory.	
	20/10	a.m.	S.H.2. moved to HEDAUVILLE - Saw St PAUL & observed him the remarks of Vet Offr. Commander re the Condition of his animals & of 6/53 including horsemanship & his V.O. in charge.	
		p.m.	Went to Rail Head treat remounts - met D.D.R. train very late, unable to wait as I am due to lecture at HAVERNAS at 5.30 p.m.	
HEDAUVILLE	21/10	a.m.	Inspected A B & D 153 Bde - A Bally fair. B Bally poor. D Bally good. Also inspected over 6 horses to be evacuated in debility from the latter. Also inspected 16th Rding Regt. Condition & animals Good, also M Cable Section.	
		p.m.	Visited Dist Force, also DnVS stripped Remounts. V.O. came to air Paris Returns.	

Army Form C. 2118.

WAR DIARY
or
INTELLIGENCE SUMMARY.
(Erase heading not required.)

Instructions regarding War Diaries and Intelligence Summaries are contained in F. S. Regs., Part II. and the Staff Manual respectively. Title pages will be prepared in manuscript.

Place	Date	Hour	Summary of Events and Information	Remarks and references to Appendices
HEDAUVILLE	22/4/16	am	Routine office - despatches weekly summary. pm - Routine	
	23/4/16	am	Visited M.V.S. & inspected horses for evacuation - Despatches weekly returns	
		pm	Visited MARTINSART & had a look round.	
	24/4/16	am	Inspected the transport lines of No. 3 Mountain Bty at FORCEVILLE - Condition of animals fair, but have improved since last inspection. Also inspected horse pen lines of D/173 Bde R.F.A.	
		pm	Routine	
	25/4/16	am	Inspected 108th Inf Bde. Sn. G. Coy. Condition of animals good - Shoeing & general satisfactory	
			" 107th " " " " " " "	
			" 13th R. J. R. " " " " " "	
			Visited Art. Forge & saw Farriers Class at work.	
		pm	Office - routine	
	26/4/16	am	Inspected transport animals of the "W. Riding Regt." which had just arrived in this area, returning the 1/6 W.R. Regt. General condition satisfactory. Looked around horse lines in HEDAUVILLE WOOD - D/172 Bde R.F.A. just moved in from TOUTENCOURT & gone into the WOOD.	

Place	Date	Hour	Summary of Events and Information	Remarks and references to Appendices
HEDAUVILLE	26/6	pm	Inspected 8th & 10th R.I.R. billets & arrival at LEAUVILLERS — Condition of animals very good — Spoke with O.C. Bn & train re his V.O. & whether is any pony satisfactory — Received favourable report. Cpl (?) 8102. had the linseed which comes up to being distributed. Recommended that he buy quantity to be small & should not be issued in a wet damp/5 hours in foot condition — Also asked Q. D.H.Q. re ques[tion] of L.S. for 16th Div. & dressing of appointment to Sid & lock shoes to allowed NCOs' but holding my appointment (centenary) indent for Remount. Office — Submitted forthnightly indent for Remounts.	
	27/6	am	Visited PUCHVILLERS — Inspected Camp of 51st Cavalry who have just come back from training — Horses looking well after a harm time. Inspected the Div. Amm. Col. — General all round improvement, especially in their lee shelter has reported on ahead by me a month ago — Called at W.V.S. at HARPONVILLE & inspected — Saw 3 Clever old had just arrived.	
	28/6	am	Inspected C. Batty 173" Bde.Am...h have improved since last inspection but are still room for more improvement. Inspected 173.B.A.C.	

WAR DIARY or INTELLIGENCE SUMMARY

Army Form C. 2118.

Place	Date	Hour	Summary of Events and Information	Remarks and references to Appendices
HEDAUVILLE	28/10/16	a.m.	The condition of the animals of this Unit — many were in need of recognition. In a shower report was submitted by me a month ago — Inspected D. Batty 72nd Bde — Condition of animals fair only — BSR's & horse Coan W.S.D.I.G. — Took his word A & B Subgr 153 Bde & also 153 B.A.C. He was very satisfied with the condition of the horses.	
	29/10/16	a.m.	Inspected A Batty 173 Bde R.F.A. — Condition shown "fair", but the Batty has had no horses evacuated for debility for the last few casualties. The watering question is difficult. The horses usually having to go to MANCY — being 2 hours shortage from watering alone like several hours daily. Inspected B & D Subgr 173rd at FORCEVILLE — Condition satisfactory. Some difficulty with water, not sufficient in FORCEVILLE for all animals located there.	
	30/10/16	a.m.	Inspected transport animals of 10th R. Irish Res & 11th R.I.R. Condition Good. Inspected 163rd Veterinary Called attention of O.C. to the numbers of cases of Iosic deaths due thirst.	
		p.m.	Inspected Animals for evacuation at the 48th Mob. V.S. Inspected 134th Bde	

WAR DIARY
or
INTELLIGENCE SUMMARY.
(Erase heading not required.)

Army Form C. 2118.

Place	Date	Hour	Summary of Events and Information	Remarks and references to Appendices
HEDAUVILLE	30/7/16	pm	18th Army led at his request at Div H.Q. in change. The condition of the horses is less satisfactory than it was about a fortnight ago. They require a get-back on arrival in moving from FORCEVILLE to HARPONVILLE during the hay rain. Arranged to inspect again in a week's time before reporting to H.Q.	

Clive Webb
Major
A.V.S. 36th Div.

WAR DIARY or INTELLIGENCE SUMMARY

Army Form C. 2118.

ADUS 36 Vol 8

Place	Date	Hour	Summary of Events and Information	Remarks and references to Appendices
HEDAUVILLE	1/5/16	a.m.	Routine – Visited Sis' Forge at VARENNES – also HdQrs of Dis' Train at LEALVILLERS	
		p.m.	Office – Visited VARENNES & FORCEVILLE	
	2/5/16	a.m.	Inspected 122 Hy Batty – Condition shown f "B" Batty good – horses have improved considerably since my last inspection – Condition f "B" Batty not so satisfactory – On the whole animals poor – Examined & horses for "Debility". Inspected veterinary troughs at FORCEVILLE. Rain is insufficient water to feed them – At present tin into supply of FORCEVILLE is inadequate, & many troughs have still to be [?] achieved. The multi is now making competition. Attended spoke at the Dis' Train to Judge in the making competition. 15/4 How Bde – Condition shown f "B" Batty good – There horses have improved considerably since my last inspection – Condition f "B" Batty not so satisfactory	
	3/5/16	a.m.	Inspected Johnny boots – will result as under – 21 Hy Batty – Condition Varnied very good – on the grass not look as if Wormed – better Carmore hook 108 Hy Batty – Condition very good "C" Batty 154 Bde R.F.A. – Horses & mules once last inspection general condition my be called "fair". Submitted Inspection Reports to HQ Div Arty.	

WAR DIARY
or
INTELLIGENCE SUMMARY.
(Erase heading not required.)

Army Form C. 2118.

Place	Date	Hour	Summary of Events and Information	Remarks and references to Appendices
HÉDAUVILLE	3/5/16	p.m.	Visited MARTINSART dressing st. V.O. to see new cases.	
	4/5/16	a.m.	Visited 152 Hy Batty at VARENNES — Just arrived from England — Put Capt HAYTER i/c Vet: Duties & arranged to inspect: transport. Visited Mobile Vet: Sec & gave instructions to O.C. re arrival & distribution of Remounts today.	
		p.m.	Incl. Remounts at Railhead (69) — Saw D.D.R. Fourth Army	
	5/5/16	a.m.	Inspected 152 Hy Batty — Condition of horses good but soft — Shoeing very much behindhand — Submitted report — Visited HQ. 9 Hy Bty I.Sd.	
		p.m.	Gave lecture at the Artillery School HAVERNAS.	
	6/5/16	a.m.	Visited MARTINSART to investigate result of enemy aeroplane bombs which caused 14 casualties amongst animals of F.K. twos two batteries — Best result — 3 killed outright — 6 destroyed — 5 wounded to be evacuated.	
		p.m.	Visited Railhead to examine animals (very emaciated) to M.V.S.	
	7/5/16	a.m.	Inspected "B" & "C" Battys 153 Bde R.F.A Submitted favourable report on both.	
		p.m.	Office — Visited MARTINSART to inspect water supply — also before a more suitable site (w horse lines) in the village.	
	8/5/16	a.m. p.m.	Routine	

Army Form C. 2118.

WAR DIARY
or
INTELLIGENCE SUMMARY.
(Erase heading not required.)

Instructions regarding War Diaries and Intelligence Summaries are contained in F. S. Regs., Part II. and the Staff Manual respectively. Title pages will be prepared in manuscript.

Place	Date	Hour	Summary of Events and Information	Remarks and references to Appendices
HEDAUVILLE	9/5	am	Visited Div Forge and inspected work going on — Inspected 13 Rounds just arrived for 9th R. Munster Fus. — Reported to re-inspt — slots of reins at Tu Triphe who being operation in — to hell we stop in Progress & recommend Probation until further orders — both O.C. Div Train recommended two trying to put now grazing to supplement — Corpoms Upoer horses — the H.D. we very anxious of the hey purchases	
	10/5	am	Attended Conference at the Office of DADVS Pont't Army Inspected M.V.S. — also 154th Bde Am Col — Tromos & toiles in very poor condition Visited MARTINSART to see new site of horse lines. Inspected lines & newly arrived Infantry Transport at HEDAUVILLE	
	11/5	am	Inspected C/173 & B/172 Batts — Condition of the horses of the former poor and of the latter satisfactory	
		pm	Visited FORCEVILLE & inspected am horses of 122nd Field Coy & also of R.J.K. — Made eng n'ries into the arrangements for a better water supply —	
	12/5	am	Inspected animals for evacuation at the M.V.S. — Visited PUCHVILLIERS — had a talk with the Dr. Stag who again complained about his V.O.	

Army Form C. 2118.

WAR DIARY
or
INTELLIGENCE SUMMARY.
(Erase heading not required.)

Instructions regarding War Diaries and Intelligence Summaries are contained in F. S. Regs., Part II. and the Staff Manual respectively. Title pages will be prepared in manuscript.

Place	Date	Hour	Summary of Events and Information	Remarks and references to Appendices
HEDAUVILLE	12/16	a.m.	Enquired into the matter & came to the conclusion that there are faults on both sides & that it is advisable to change the VO as he does not hit it off. Left several of the officers.	
		p.m.	Inspected No 1 & 3 Coys A.S.C. Transport & horses for debility from her log. General condition of animals very good.	
	13/16	a.m.	DDS Fourth Army came to see horses for casting — despatched weekly summary.	
		p.m.	Office.	
	14/16	a.m.	Visited HARPONVILLE & TOUTENCOURT — Inspected C & D Batts 172 Bde R.F.A — Their batteries have not changed all the poor horses with the Column, as their condition is good.	
		p.m.	Routine — horses & remt units in HEDAUVILLE.	
	16/16	a.m.	Visited units in FORCEVILLE - VARENNES & HEDAUVILLE —	
		p.m.	Inspected 2 Secs 18pdrs & 1 Sec 4.7 (Hvy) first arrival VARENNES. belonging to 49 Div Artillery — Horses in good condition — Placed Capt HAYTER in Vet Charge — Inspected all vets troughs & enquired into water supply at	

WAR DIARY or INTELLIGENCE SUMMARY

Army Form C. 2118.

Place	Date	Hour	Summary of Events and Information	Remarks and references to Appendices
HEDAUVILLE	15th	pm	at VARENNES & FORCEVILLE — Inspected 2 sections of '½" to Rising Fields R.E. just arrived at HEDAUVILLE. Placed Capt. McCLINTOCK in Vet. charge.	
	16th	am	Inspected 108 Bde M.G. Coy. Arranged to transfer 2 horses. Inspected Hd. Qrs. & hrs. 7th Bde Bicycle Coy. under instructions from G.O.C. Submitted a report to the effect that their condition was quite satisfactory. Submitted a report to A.D.V.S. including an observed by return, recommending an increase. Showed to Q. who noted me to hold it up as the question of supplementary by feeding was under consideration.	
		pm	Inspected A Battery 153 Bde. Condition of horses very good. This battery lately here are very well supervised & the credit of the horses great credit. Visited MARTINSART. See the location of new Units in the WOOD.	
	17th	am	Inspected animals for evacuation at the M.V.S. Evacuated 18 cases of debility from 154 Bde.	
		pm	Inspected 51/153 Bde. Practically no evacuations for debility have taken place from this Unit & the condition of the animals is now good. Visited MARTINSART. Inspected several cases with the V.O.	

WAR DIARY or INTELLIGENCE SUMMARY

Army Form C. 2118.

Place	Date	Hour	Summary of Events and Information	Remarks and references to Appendices
HEDAUVILLE	18/5/16	a.m.	Inspected 16th R. Irish Fus. at LEALVILLERS – Condition of animals good. Saw I.O. of 14th R.I.R. – Inspected a horse for Castings. Called to see the S.S.O. re the question of Forging – Rewrote supply at VARENNES now open –	
		p.m.	Visited HARPONVILLE to inspect 154 B.A.C. & pick out cases of debility recovered from Veterinary ch – Inspected 17 H.D. taken over from 29th Divn – Instructed that 1 horse to remain as an L.D. and another to evacuate for debility. Saw me.	
	19/5/16	a.m.	Visited MARTINSART & inspected animals of 191st & 150th 2nd Corps R.E. also some animals of the 16th R.I.R.	
		p.m.	Examined 7 men from Inf. Batt'lns at the Vet. Dist. Forge as to their fitness for the appointment of Shoeingsmith & Coldshoers – Passed 4 men as Shoeing Smiths & 3 men as Coldshoers –	
	20/5/16	a.m.	Routine – p.m. visited MARTINSART	
	21/5/16	a.m.	Inspected 73rd B.A.C. & advised 7 horses for evacuation for debility –	
		p.m.	Lectured at the Army Artillery School –	
	22/5/16	a.m.	Saw A.D.V.S. 32nd Divn & letters re the question of slaughter horses. Office.	
		p.m.	Visited LEALVILLERS to inspect some horses of Div. Train.	

Army Form C. 2118.

WAR DIARY
or
INTELLIGENCE SUMMARY

(Erase heading not required.)

Instructions regarding War Diaries and Intelligence Summaries are contained in F. S. Regs., Part II. and the Staff Manual respectively. Title Pages will be prepared in manuscript.

Place	Date	Hour	Summary of Events and Information	Remarks and references to Appendices
HEDAUVILLE	23/5/16	a.m.	Spent the day at PROHVILLERS going through the Shoffleur B.A.C. horses & viewing same as Remounts to this Division & also to the 48th & 29th Divisions.	
	24/5/16	a.m.	Issued Remounts from Shoffleur B.A.C. horses to the 49th Divn — Inspected the first Cavalry — Condition of horses satisfactory.	
		p.m.	Visited Units in HEDAUVILLE — FORCEVILLE & VARENNES.	
	25/5/16	a.m.	Inspected A/154 Batty. Condition of horses good — Also 14th W.Riding Regt. Condition of horses good with the exception of 2 or 3 remounts just received — Inspected 6th K.O.Y.L.I. just arrived in this area — condition of animals very good — Also inspected Hqrs Section D.A.C. half come to HEDAUVILLE. The condition of attrained this section continues to be satisfactory — Called attention to the necessity for removing hair driest. Manure not heaping up behind the lines.	
		p.m.	Visited FORCEVILLE & VARENNES	
	26/5/16	a.m.	Inspected Section of A.C. & Batty 247/Sh & 17 Fn (49th Divn) located at VARENNES accompanied by the V.O. — Horses all in good condition — Also inspected 115th R.Lancashire & 109th Field Ambulance — Result Satisfactory.	
		p.m.	Visited MARTINSART.	
	27/5/16	a.m.	Inspected following units with result as under —	

2449 Wt. W14957/M90 750,000 1/16 J.B.C. & A. Forms/C.2118/12.

WAR DIARY
or
INTELLIGENCE SUMMARY

Army Form C. 2118.

(Erase heading not required.)

Place	Date	Hour	Summary of Events and Information	Remarks and references to Appendices
HEDAUVILLE	27/5/16	a.m.	C/173 Batty R.F.A. — Condition of animals not yet satisfactory in spite of exchanges with surplus B.A.C. horses — Horses are backward in their work, due I think to want of proper grooming. There is not the supervision in this Batty that there should be.	
			B/153 Batty R.F.A. — Improvement maintained — recommended more exercise — Horses carry yd by bellies but not much muscle.	
			C/153 Batty R.F.A. — Great improvement — condition good — Horses well groomed and exercised. In balcony feeding, recovery very satisfactory.	
			Hd Qrs & No.1 Sec Sigl Coy — condition of animals satisfactory, but state of lines not so. Difficulty in finding fatigue parties for repairs to lines.	
		p.m.	Inspected "B" Echelon D.A.C. — condition of animals satisfactory — Also inspected the Mobile Vet Sec.	
	28/5/16	a.m.	Office — Inspected 3rd Hussars Regt ordered destruction of 2 horses (London Gazette).	
		p.m.	Visited TOUTENCOURT — Spoke to Adjutant 172nd Bde R.F.A. re leave of R.V.C. Sergeants. Some improvement which had been reported to me.	

WAR DIARY
or
INTELLIGENCE SUMMARY

(Erase heading not required.)

Army Form C. 2118.

Place	Date	Hour	Summary of Events and Information	Remarks and references to Appendices
HERAUVILLE	29/5/16	a.m.	Inspected the following units as under:—	
			D/172 Batty. – Condition of animals fair to poor. Appear to be recovering from effects of attention – but there is still room for improvement.	
			B/173 Batty. – Condition of animals very good – Quite one of the best battys in the Division so far – as the present condition of its horse is concerned.	
			A/153 Batty. – Condition of animals fair to good.	
			C/173 Batty. – Good.	
			Received complaints with regard to the oats – Found them to contain a large percentage of wheat – Otherwise the supply was good. Delivery arrangements in Acheville have been working satisfactorily up to to-day, but has now cut off from ACHEUX today owing to the shelling of the cattle place at the source of supply.	
	30/5/16	a.m.	Visited H.V.S. and arranged for disposal of some cast/slim horses – Got forage and arranged ammunition for forward lines.	
		p.m.	Confini	

Place	Date	Hour	Summary of Events and Information	Remarks and references to Appendices
MEDAUVILLE	31/5/16	am	Inspected No 1 & 3 Sections 37 A.C. (A Echelon) at VARENNES. Render in follow - No 1 Sec - Condition of animals fair but improving - Still a certain percentage of poor mules & also horses especially horses recently transferred from B.A.C. Stable management supervision appears to be good - No 3 Sec - Condition of animals good with the exception of a few old mules	

Alive Wolff
Major AVC
A.D.V.S. 36th Divn

WAR DIARY or INTELLIGENCE SUMMARY

Army Form C. 2118.

ADVS 36(a)   Vol 9 of June

Place	Date	Hour	Summary of Events and Information	Remarks and references to Appendices
HEDAUVILLE	1/6/16	am.	Routine	
		pm.	Visited Railhead & letter over and arrange distribution of 32 remounts.	
	2/6/16	Am.	Inspected transport horses of 4th S.R.: 6th: 7th Battn W. Riding (147 Inf. Bde. 49th Divn.) also Amb. Coy. Arrived in this Divl area yesterday. Arranged Vety attendance (Capt. D. KINNOCHIE) — Also inspected 8th & 10th Battns R.I.R. — horses & DDVS for 14th Army — look for a V.O. from the 49th Divn as there as was an infants and no attestings side of the 49th Divn in this area — Separated horse boxes (for self and O.C. Mobile Vet. Section) at 4th Army Artillery school.	
	3/6/16	Am.	Inspected C.S. waggon horses [illegible] Have just arrived in this Divl area — Condition of horses good — Arranged Vety attendance	
		pm.	Visited MARTINSART	
	4/6/16	Am.	Routine — Inspected abs'ty of A.S.C. (49th Div.) — lot of horses —	
		pm.	Inspected 8th W. York Regt (49th Divn) recentrainment — showing in a very bad state.	

WAR DIARY or INTELLIGENCE SUMMARY

Army Form C. 2118.

Place	Date	Hour	Summary of Events and Information	Remarks and references to Appendices
HEDAUVILLE	5/6	a.m.	Visited Prof. Vet. Sec. & inspected horses and suffering horses traced evacuation of one charger under treatment for suspected mange to be evacuated. Inspected 11th & 13th R.H.B. — Condition of former good — latter not satisfactory as regards H.D. horses.	
		p.m.	Routine.	
	6/6	a.m.	Routine — received wire from DDVS reporting that a horse belonging to H.Q. 173rd Bde inoculated in the C/md. had reacted to mallein — Forwarded preliminary report re same. Made arrangements for testing.	
		p.m.	Visited MARTINSART & saw Adjutant 173rd Bde R.F.A. re testing.	
	7/6	a.m.	Inspected 16 & C Batty 172nd Bde R.F.A. at TOUTENCOURT — Condition of 0/172 good, B/172 fair & good — This batty still has a certain number of poor horses which require feeding up — Saw 2 horse backs pulled & men from Wound galls etc. sufficience —	
		p.m.	Inspected 247th Bde R.F.A (D of Div) lean & half. at VARENNES — Condition of horses of the 2 Field Batteries very good & horses very well kept. — Condition of Howitzer Bty not so good.	

2449 Wt. W14957/M90 750,000 1/16 J.B.C. & A. Forms/C.2118/12.

WAR DIARY or INTELLIGENCE SUMMARY

Army Form C. 2118.

Place	Date	Hour	Summary of Events and Information	Remarks and references to Appendices
HEDAUVILLE	8/6/16	a.m.	Visited lines of 1/52nd Hy Batty going to England - by Lt. V.O. that the horses had a very bad state except for animals - came to conclusion that the horses of this Batty are being neglected - no attempt at cleaning lines, insufficient men, stables & roadways being wet - Return report to H.Q. 9th C.H.A. Group. Visited M.V.S re animal distressed & fallen at the Base	
		p.m.	Office - Reported to HQ 9th CHA Gp re care of horses in A/153 - arranged inspection	
	9/6/16	a.m.	Inspected A/153 Batty - Horses in fair good condition & no further figures of their shoes - Inspected horses of HQ 173 Bde R.F.A. Vellinin[?] yesterday - no reaction -	
		p.m.	Routine	
	10/6/16	a.m.	Routine	
		p.m.	Visited A.D.V.S. 32nd Divn & arranged V.S. attendance for E Staffs Hy Artily at SENLIS & WARENNES	
	11/6/16	a.m.	Inspected 246th Bde R.F.A. (49th Divn) (which arrived at HEDAUVILLE yesterday) - arranged Vety attendance -	
		p.m.	Went to a lecture on the Royal Baths - Despatched weekly returns etc.	

WAR DIARY or INTELLIGENCE SUMMARY

Army Form C. 2118.

Place	Date	Hour	Summary of Events and Information	Remarks and references to Appendices
HEDAUVILLE	12/6/16	am	Inspected horses in evacuation at the M.V.S. - Saw a horse admitted from 108th Hy Batty on Demotitis. Said I considered very suspicious of mange. Reported same to D.D.V.S. & called for a report from the V.O. of 108th Hy Batty. Visited the lines of 5/9a6 Batty. Will arrived 2 days ago & arranged to inspect their horses tomorrow.	
		pm	Returned office.	
	13/6/16	am	Inspected 5/9a6 Batty - Horses in very good condition. Visited LEAVILLERS - Saw Lt. Col. Train & V.O. - Met Capt. HAYTER at VARENNES & arranged for inoculating 152" Hy Batty tomorrow.	
		pm	Office - Wrote ADVS 49 Div re Vet arrangements during Offensive - Asked Q to change lines of 152 Hy Batty. Arranged Vet attendance for 466 Co, RSC. Just arrived.	
	14/6/16	am	Inoculated 152" Hy Batty recently arrived from England.	
		pm	Attended Q Conference & took details re Offensive. Had a Conference of Vety Officers.	

Army Form C. 2118.

WAR DIARY
or
INTELLIGENCE SUMMARY
(Erase heading not required.)

Instructions regarding War Diaries and Intelligence Summaries are contained in F. S. Regs., Part II. and the Staff Manual respectively. Title Pages will be prepared in manuscript.

Place	Date	Hour	Summary of Events and Information	Remarks and references to Appendices
HEDAUVILLE	15/6/16	a.m.	Completed the mustering of 152nd Bn by R.Q.C. – no reaction from yesterday	
		p.m.	Visited MARTINSART – Selected site for advanced Vety Post.	
	16/6/16	a.m.	Inspected horses of 152nd Bty. R.C.A. – no reaction. DDR with Army came to inspect animals for casting.	
		p.m.	Sgt. removed at Sickbed – Inspected horses/reservation at the 2nd Vet. Sec.	
	17/6/16	a.m.	Routine.	
		p.m.	– Took O.C. Mobile v LIEUT. SHAW over position for the advanced post, also places for regimental v roads/for horse ambulance	
	18/6/16	a.m.	Walked round all lines in HEDAUVILLE Neue iny – worked/trs 36./Bnt. Arty.	
		p.m.	Attended a Conference at the office of DDVS with Army. Capt. A.H. WATSON. A.V.C. reported his arrival this morning from tour & sworn in as S in the 3rd Army –	
	19/6/16	a.m.	Inspected 3 French belgian horses 45.46 of the 25 Reg d'Artillerie, accompanied by the VO Litoge Auchojet – Rd forward position of	

2449 Wt. W14957/M90 750,000 1/16 J.B.C. & A. Forms/C.2118/12.

WAR DIARY
or
INTELLIGENCE SUMMARY

Army Form C. 2118.

Place	Date	Hour	Summary of Events and Information	Remarks and references to Appendices
HEDAUVILLE	19/6	a.m.	Evacuating sick, remounting them & supplying medicines.	
		p.m.	Inspected all units at FORCEVILLE - 6th R.J.R - 150 Fld Coy R.E. - 5th MN R. transp - 15th R.J.R. 463 & 466 Coys A.S.C. - 108th Fd Howitzer - 4th R.J.R - 16th R. train Train - 152nd & 2nd Coys R.E. - 9th R. train Train - 16.106th Coy R.E. - 13th & 7 Coy R.E - Visited AVELUY after division had transport-pony up but ammunition & rations.	
	20/6	a.m.	Inspected horses for evacuation at Mob. Vet. Sec - Case of superficial mange from 2 of 466 Coy A.S.C. - slight eruption under the saddle - retaining in M.V.S. for observation - several cases of pricks from barb shoeing admitted within last few days from 152nd Hy Batty. Called to see the O.C. who was away, but saw the Adjt & called his attention to the bad shoeing etc.	
		p.m.	Went to DOULLENS to try & arrange contract for carcases & hides.	
	21/6	a.m.	D.D.V.S. had a conference in my office. The A.D.V.S. of 32nd & 29th Divn attending. Capt. W. D. Connochie reported his return from leave - posted him to 172nd Bde R.A.	
		p.m.	Inspected all units in LEALVILLERS viz. M/O Hq - Div. Train - Detach'. Reserve Park. 10th R.J.R - 105th Coy R.E.	

WAR DIARY
or
INTELLIGENCE SUMMARY

Army Form C. 2118.

(Erase heading not required.)

Place	Date	Hour	Summary of Events and Information	Remarks and references to Appendices
HEDAUVILLE	22/6/16	a.m.	Visit from A.D.V.S. 32nd Divn to discuss arrangements for establishing operations	
		p.m.	Inspected M.V.S. - also 73rd Echelon stores. Condition of Mule Standings bad in spite of very hard work lately.	
	23/6/16	a.m.	M.V.S. moved to HEDAUVILLE - ordered LIEUT. SHAW to move to site of Advanced Post.	
		p.m.	Routine	
	24/6/16	a.m.	Visited Brit. Transport Camp & Advanced Vety Post.	
		p.m.	Routine	
	25/6/16	a.m.	Visited Cav. Post & MARTINSART	
		p.m.	D.D.V.S. witherby called - Inspected Mls & the Ins Pavilion Park just arrived - Inspector of 347 Batt.	
	26/6/16	a.m.	Have taken away environment in condition. Inspected horses for evacuation to the M.V.S. - Routine Office.	
		p.m.	Visited advanced Post - Arranged for collection of remounts at Rail head.	

Army Form C. 2118.

WAR DIARY
or
INTELLIGENCE SUMMARY
(Erase heading not required.)

Instructions regarding War Diaries and Intelligence Summaries are contained in F. S. Regs., Part II. and the Staff Manual respectively. Title Pages will be prepared in manuscript.

Place	Date	Hour	Summary of Events and Information	Remarks and references to Appendices
HÉDAUVILLE	27/6	a.m.	Inspected 108 Hy Batty. — Horses in good condition. All the horses in the orchards at VARENNES are in very bad condition. Said Capt-Burston who reported that B Echelon 49th Divn. had just arrived. Instructed him to take over Vet. Charge, & relieved him of B Echelon 36th R.F.A. & 149 & 170th Howitzers from this latter to Capt Wauchie — 2k 248th Bde R.F.A. (49 Divn) arrives 6 Aug — this was also kept his Train.	
		p.m.	Officer inspected nullimes horses of Bey Sec 108 Pontoon Park — No reactions.	
	28/6	a.m.	Inspected Camp 1 Divl Train at FORCEVILLE — horses about 49 Divn. Meeting over the administration than Vet Units of 49 Divn.	
		p.m.	Visited Advanced Post of Divl Transport Camp.	
	29/6	a.m.	Routine —	
		p.m.	Inspected 153 & 173 Bdes R.F.A. — Condition fair, satisfactory, catering into consideration recent weather conditions & hard work.	

WAR DIARY
INTELLIGENCE SUMMARY

Army Form C. 2118.

Place	Date	Hour	Summary of Events and Information	Remarks and references to Appendices
HÉDAUVILLE	30/6	am	Inspected 172' Bde R.F.A. — General condition of horses satisfactory — "B" Batty not so good as the remainder. Also inspected the transport lines writing of detachments from "A" & "B" Echelon S.A.C. Some of the mules & horses in very poor condition, viewing the work have been sent on detachment. Submitted report to HQ.25 36th Div. a/c's. for Return	

Andrewell
Major A.V.C.
A.D.V.S. 36th Divn.

36 Army Form C 2118.
July
ADVS 36 Dv
Vol 10

WAR DIARY or INTELLIGENCE SUMMARY
(Erase heading not required.)

Instructions regarding War Diaries and Intelligence Summaries are contained in F.S. Regs, Part II. and the Staff Manual respectively. Title Pages will be prepared in manuscript.

Place	Date	Hour	Summary of Events and Information	Remarks and references to Appendices
HEDAUVILLE	1/7/16	a.m.	Commencement of Battle – Visited Advanced Post – MARTINSART and AVELUY WOOD.	
		p.m.	Routine –	
	2/7/16	a.m.	Arranged for collection & distribution of 63 Remounts – 20 casualties from shell fire reported on the receipt of yesterday's "Strafe" – went to see Remounts – hei-DDR ADVS 49 it's Corps – gave me re latrine at my Adv. Post – Informed him I was not withdrawing my Post for the present.	
	3/7/16	a.m.	Went from ADVS Albany Street – Met him at my office & interviews Lieut-Millepine.	
		p.m.	Took ADVS round the MVS and Advanced Post – Inspected 8th & 15th R.J.R and 131st Fld Ambg R.E	
	4/7/16	a.m.	1st New transport moved from Sus Hampol Camp back to HEDAUVILLE – FOREVILLE & HARPONVILLE – Rearranged Vety Hunter – Inthess advanced Post & handed over Site, Stables & gun trench to OC 1/5 (W.R) Mt Vet Sec	
	5/7/16	a.m.	Received orders that the Division (in batteries, Engineers & Pioneers moves tomorrow to TOUTENCOURT – Handed out supplies now for evacuating purposes to the	
			RUBEMPRÉ – PUCHVILLERS, HERISSART area – Ad. Vet Sec. moves this afternoon	

WAR DIARY or INTELLIGENCE SUMMARY

Army Form C. 2118.

Place	Date	Hour	Summary of Events and Information	Remarks and references to Appendices
HEDAUVILLE	5/7/16	a.m.	1/1st (W.R.) Mob. Vet. Sec. — Handed over administration of 36 sick Artillery Engineers & Pioneers to the A.D.V.S. 49th Div. with 3 Vety. Officers viz:— CAPTAINS McCLINTOCK, CONNOCHIE & LIEUT MILLER —	
		p.m.	Completed arrangements for moving	
RUBEMPRE	6/7/16	a.m.	1/1 Sec. moved to RUBEMPRE	
		p.m.	Went to see the A.D.V.S. 49th Div. re Vety. Officers of 36th Div. Artillery and with 49th Div. and arrange before more Vety. Assistance if necessary.	
	7/7/16	a.m.	Visited MOB. VET. SEC. at TOUTENCOURT — Called on O.C. No 3 Coy A.S.C. re an(?)	
			case of a remount from M.V.S.	
		p.m.	Routine — Called here DDVS Reserve Army at RAINCHEVAL.	
	8/7/16	a.m.	Visited 109th Bde at HERISSART — Handed out the Turning of Remounts for the Division to Q. at Q's request — Have been doing the Remount work	
			of the Division for the past 9 months.	
		p.m.	Inspected all transport animals & those of the M.G. Coy & the 107th Inf. Brigade at RUBEMPRE — Condition of animals as a whole very satisfactory — Visited M.V.S. at TOUTENCOURT & arranged with O.C. re evacuation of all sick preparatory for immediate move.	

Army Form C. 2118.

WAR DIARY
or
INTELLIGENCE SUMMARY
(Erase heading not required.)

Instructions regarding War Diaries and Intelligence Summaries are contained in F. S. Regs., Part II. and the Staff Manual respectively. Title Pages will be prepared in manuscript.

Place	Date	Hour	Summary of Events and Information	Remarks and references to Appendices
RUBEMPRE	9/7/16	am. pm.	Routine - Office - weekly returns	
BERNAVILLE	10/7/16	am.	HHQ moved to BERNAVILLE - The Division moved to BERNAVILLE - FIENVILLERS - BEZAINCOURT area - Asst. Vet. Sec. to BEAUMETZ - Wired A.D.V.S. 49th Div. for the return of Lieut. PAUL on account of the Field Corps R.E. and U.K. S.A.A. Sect. D.A.C. returning from the 49th to the 36th Div.	
"	11/7/16	pm. am. pm.	Visited BEAUVAL to see hints collecting time for the night viz - SOMEVAL - D.A.C. and 3 Field Corps. Saw the V.O. 49th MW.S. and gave him instructions re moving Brecyne HHQ moved to BLARINGHAM and the Division to the BLARINGHAM - WARDRECQUES -	
BLARINGHAM	12/7/16	am. pm.	RACQUINGHEM - CAMPAGNE area. Inspected S.H.Q. Animals - Inspected Site of Billets for the Mob. Vet. Sec. arriving to day Visited units at CAMPAGNE viz - R.E. Corps & Field Ambulances	
TILQUES	13/7/16	am. pm.	S.H.Q. moved to TILQUES and the Division to the TILQUES area Visited the following units - S.A.A. Sec. D.A.C. (NORDAUSQUES) - 107 Coy HQ. (ZANNES) - 202 Coy. A.S.C. (HELLEBROUCQ) - Railhead (WATTEN) - H.Q. R.E. (SERQUES) - Lieut. PAUL A.V.C. who had some astray en route from BERNAVILLE to TILQUES turned up from ABBEVILLE !!	

WAR DIARY or INTELLIGENCE SUMMARY

Army Form C. 2118.

Place	Date	Hour	Summary of Events and Information	Remarks and references to Appendices
TILQUES	14/7/16	a.m.	Took LIEUT PAUL A.V.C. to NORDAUSQUES & put him in charge of the S.A.A.S.C. and 107th Inf Bde including 2/2 Coy A.S.C. and 110th Field Ambulance - Inspected S.A.A. Sec. (practically "B" Echelon) - Animals looking very "fine" as the result of hard work at HARPRINGHEM and the journey here. Mules & horses sent by "A" Echelon nothing specially poor - evidently picked out their worst - sent over to B Echelon - Earmarked 3 horses & 2 mules for debility - det of C amp & Mules very good - Animal standard soon pick up. Visited 2/2 Coy A.S.C. - No casualties on the line of march - Also visited the 108th & 110th Field Ambulances at WESTROSE who had no casualties to report. Met LIEUT SHAW M.C. & directed him to make his H.Q.s with H.Q.s 2 Coy R.E. and to take b/cg charge of the 108th Inf Bde including A.S.C. Coy, Field Ambce, H.Q.2bg & Field Coys R.E. and 16th R.I.R. (?).	
	15/7/16	p.m.	Visit from DDVS Kemmel Army who gave me general instructions & procedure.	
		a.m.	Visited Q.R.hain in at ZUDAUSQUES - Saw the transport of Animals - Nothing real or had suffered no casualties on the line of march. Water supply & village not good.	

Army Form C. 2118.

WAR DIARY
or
INTELLIGENCE SUMMARY

(Erase heading not required.)

Instructions regarding War Diaries and Intelligence Summaries are contained in F.S. Regs., Part II. and the Staff Manual respectively. Title Pages will be prepared in manuscript.

Place	Date	Hour	Summary of Events and Information	Remarks and references to Appendices
TILQUES	15/7/16	a.m.	Arrived — 1 & 2 small ponds — 1 very small and muddy & unfit for animals, the other a larger clean, & trenches to water & suitable if troughs were erected. Recommended to T.O. that failing troughs, detachment be moved & animals not led into pond. Called at D. 109 & Inf Bde H.Qrs at QUELMES also on No. 1 Co. 109 & H.G. Coy — no casualties from the time of march to-port — the other units — all horses in QUELMES — watertroughs — a large pond with sandy bottom — water fairly clear & animals feeding by animal.	
		p.m.	Office — weekly returns — drafters & orders for Divisional re Changes of N.O.s	
	16/7/16	a.m.	Accompanied A.Q.M.G. in the inspection of the 16 R.J.R. (Pioneer) — Condition of animals satisfactory, but general turn-out — shoeing — harness not-hogged, grooming indifferent and shoeing very bad.	
		p.m.	Routine	
	17/7/16	a.m.	Inspected horse lines of RESO, at SETQUES — Condition of animals good, also shoeing — Site of Camp & water supply very good	

WAR DIARY
or
INTELLIGENCE SUMMARY

(Erase heading not required.)

Army Form C. 2118.

Place	Date	Hour	Summary of Events and Information	Remarks and references to Appendices
TILQUES	17/7/16	a.m.	Inspected 11th R. Sco: Fus at SETQUES — Condition Général very good — No casualties in the three Companies up here — Camp rates Supply very good. Inspected 10th R. Inns: Fus at ACQUIN — Condition Général — Camp, and horse lines supply good — No casualties in line Général.	
		p.m.	Inspected H.Qrs Div: see beyond Coy — Condition Général very good — Called attention to the absence of eye fringes which are very necessary in winter —	
	18/7/16	a.m.	Inspected the following units with results as under — 121 Coy R.E. — Condition Général good — Site of Camp & rate Supply good. 122 Coy R.E. — Condition in the whole good, but — a few very poor animals — Recommended 1 mule for destln — Several cases of rope galls — Informed O.C. that these things not occur with proper attention. Site of Camp rates supply good.	
			150th Coy R.E. — Condition Général good — Evacuated 2 mules for debility & 1 ulcer heel — shoeing not up to date.	
		p.m.	Sent O.C. N.V.S. report about the admission of 1 case of mange from No: Coy A.S.C. Supply Co.	

WAR DIARY
or
INTELLIGENCE SUMMARY

Army Form C. 2118.

Place	Date	Hour	Summary of Events and Information	Remarks and references to Appendices
TILQUES	15/7/16	pm	Inspected some of ordered evacuation - also 1 horse belonging to 48th M.V.S. with suspected mange - Visited No 23 Vety Hospital at ST OMER & had a look round	
	19/7/16	am	Visited Hd Qrs of all Adj Stns - saw Lt Col? & gave them instructions re evacuation of sick etc - Visited 71st & 14th Batts at CORMETTE - saw Lt Col? arranged Vety attendance	
			Office - Received intimation re move of Divison - Issued necessary instructions	
	20/7/16	am	Routine - Inspected horse for evacuation in the M.V.S. - Reconnaissance from No 3 Coy A.S.C.	
		pm	Routine	
ESQUELBECQ	27/7/16	am	H.Q. moved to ESQUELBECQ - M.V.S. to LEDRINGHEM	
		pm	Reported move to DDVS - Instructions O.C. M.V.S. re visiting units etc - LEDRINGHEM to WORMHOUDT	
	29/7/16	am	Went over to BAILLEUL to see ADVS 20th Div re location of his MVS, & in particular, in preparation to this Divi's move to that area - 48th M.V.S. moved to CROIX ROUGE	

Army Form C. 2118.

WAR DIARY
or
INTELLIGENCE SUMMARY

(Erase heading not required.)

Place	Date	Hour	Summary of Events and Information	Remarks and references to Appendices
MONT NOIR	23/7/16	a.m.	D.H.Q. moved to MONT NOIR — M.V.S. to pt S.8.B.9.9.(SL 28) —	
		p.m.	D.D.V.S. 2nd Army came to D.H.Q. & gave me instructions re evacuation of sick etc. Issued instructions re Vety charges	
BAILLEUL	24/7/16	a.m.	Ownrd my office to BAILLEUL as being more Central for settling amml limits —	
		p.m.	Held a Conference of Vety Officers and arranged duties etc.	
	25/7/16	a.m.	Went to Raithead & met Remounts & arrange distribution — Major Heint. L. Sullivan Vet. V Corps Hd Qrs Group and gave him instructions re Rehorsing etc.	
		p.m.	Inspected 173rd Bde R.F.A. — Animals have fallen off considerably in condition since my last inspection at HEDAUVILLE — due to exceptionally hard work during the first phase of Gen Offensive and the need up to this ann— Site of Camps & note Supply satisfactory — Shoeing satisfactory — In 3 were obliged make a great difference then appearance of left at real —	
	26/7/16	a.m.	Inspected & re classified some horses in the Anti Aircraft arm— range Contracts. Thus ' Cav	
		p.m.	Returne office	

WAR DIARY
or
INTELLIGENCE SUMMARY

Army Form C. 2118.

Place	Date	Hour	Summary of Events and Information	Remarks and references to Appendices
AMEUL	27/6	a.m.	Inspected A & D Batty. 72 Bde R.F.A. — Marked falling off in condition since last inspection. Evacuated 2 horses from A & 5 from D Batty. for stabling. Still number of animals remaining not fit for immediate work — will require rest & good feeding to put them round. Submitted report to H.Q. 5th Div Arty. and Bdy G.O.C.	
			for Routine Office.	
	28/6	a.m.	Inspected following units with results under — 108. 9th Ambce. — Animals in excellent condition — Ditto Camp & Supply Sect. — Shewing signs — too many horses with one groom — feet.	
			109. 9th Ambce. — 110. 9th Ambce. — Same remarks apply as above, excepting that the feet of animals of the 109th did not attract special attention from being overgrown.	
			56. Div Tr. & Coy. — Condition of animal good with a few exceptions.	
			for Routine Office. — ADVS visiting Callow.	

Army Form C. 2118.

WAR DIARY
or
INTELLIGENCE SUMMARY
(Erase heading not required.)

Place	Date	Hour	Summary of Events and Information	Remarks and references to Appendices
BAILLEUL	29/7/16	am	Looked for a car in the 27th Inst [?] to-day. It was cancelled at the last moment by Q on the grounds that the place to which I had said I was proceeding was only 2 to 3 miles away. Had arranged transport several times at DRANOUTRE & LOCRE — Show the absurdity of this version of the statement. Of course I protested strongly against the treatment meted out to me — he refused to admit my claim to the use of a car, so asked to see the Brit. Commander — Inspected 2nd Coy A.S.C. — Horses in excellent condition — St George's transport Supply Inspected detachment of 39' Reserve Park — Certain things which need remedies — showing potentials for travel caution. Inspected the M.M.S. and also marching cases for evacuation. Brought over new road to T₃ Q1, Q2, A.S.C. re details to be returned to its limit, as I thought a foot case of debility for Kentani. Medical interviews with the Brit. Commander re the question of motor cars.	

Army Form C. 2118.

WAR DIARY or **INTELLIGENCE SUMMARY**
(Erase heading not required.)

Place	Date	Hour	Summary of Events and Information	Remarks and references to Appendices
BAILLEUL	30/6	a.m.	Inspected the following units:— C/172 Batty — Horses looking very fine — have lost enormously in condition since my last inspection at BEAUVILLE, due to exceptionally hard work during the first phase of the offensive. Hard work on "front end". Three long tracked black horses Canadian/American horses — Evacuated 3 horses exceptionally debilitated. A/151 — The same remarks apply as above — Evacuated 11 debility cases. No 3 Sec S.T.A.C. — Condition of animals fair to good — As I have remarked before with reference to the S.T.A.C. the mules are at a very uneven lot. Gall ridges very — the big lorries are being very difficult to get into condition. Evacuated 4 debility cases, 1 old standing, and 2 harness mule (mange) — Observed distribution of one of the two mules and Cast the other.	

2449 Wt. W14957/M90 750,000 1/16 J.B.C. & A. Forms/C.2118/12.

WAR DIARY or INTELLIGENCE SUMMARY

Army Form C. 2118.

Instructions regarding War Diaries and Intelligence Summaries are contained in F. S. Regs., Part II. and the Staff Manual respectively. Title Pages will be prepared in manuscript.

(Erase heading not required.)

Place	Date	Hour	Summary of Events and Information	Remarks and references to Appendices
BAILLEUL	30/76	p.m.	Asked to see the A.P.M's dog. Suspected of Rabies. Found the dog suffering from several cataract, foul & congested membranes. Also very snappy and dangerous to handle. Gave orders for the dog to be secured tied up inside a stable for 10 days	
	31/76	a.m.	Received a wire from G.H.Q. to say that A.P.M's dog had been destroyed. Saw the A.P.M. who explained that the dog & been at him & he had therefore destroyed it. I removed the brain & placed it in pure Glycerine. The A.P.M, a Belgian officer & interpreter and a servant, all of whom had been bitten proceeded to Paris for anti-rabic treatment. Taking the brain with them	
		p.m.	Inspected the 153 Bde R.F.A. with results as under — A/153 Batty. — Horses have fallen off very much in condition since last inspection more so than other batteries inspected up to date — Evacuated 5 h debility. B/153 Batty — Condition of horses good — Very few poor ones — Men seem strong. No hard work marching very satisfactory. Evacuated 1 debility & 1 suspected mange case —	

Army Form C. 2118.

WAR DIARY
or
INTELLIGENCE SUMMARY
(Erase heading not required.)

Instructions regarding War Diaries and Intelligence Summaries are contained in F. S. Regs., Part II. and the Staff Manual respectively. Title Pages will be prepared in manuscript.

Place	Date	Hour	Summary of Events and Information	Remarks and references to Appendices
BAILLEUL	31/7/16	pm	B/153 – Condition of horses satisfactory – but to "round" as they were but are in hard condition. 2/153 – Condition of horses fair – Lines & billeting arrangements of all batteries satisfactory.	

Amwell
Major
C.R.A. 36' Divn

2449. Wt. W14957/M90 750,000 1/16 J.B.C. & A. Forms/C.2118/12.

WAR DIARY
or
INTELLIGENCE SUMMARY

(Erase heading not required.)

Army Form C. 2118.

VOL 11

D.V.S. AUG 1916 ULSTER DIVISION

Place	Date	Hour	Summary of Events and Information	Remarks and references to Appendices
BAILLEUL	1/8/16	a.m.	Routine — Office. Forwarded recommendations to Q re precautionary measures in connection with the one suspected rabies in APM's dog.	
		pm	Inspected following units:—	
	2/8/16	am	Hd Qrs Div T.M.C. — Condition of animals generally, especially mules, very good — marked improvement since my last inspection. Supervision in this unit very thorough. Submitted Inspection report to HQ Div Arty & copy to Q. 107th Inf Bde — Inspected all animals of battalions and MG. Coy — general condition of animals very good indeed but shoeing greatly at fault & shoeing as follows — Animals not shod up to date, feet not reduced to proper proportions, then shod — MG. Coy without shoeing smith of any kind at the present moment — distributed rpt to Bde A.D. stops to Q	
	3/8/16	pm	Routine — Office — DDVS paid a visit —	
		am	Inspected the following units —	
			15/17D — Condition good & fair — Have lost condition like other batteries inspected to date — Evacuated 2 cases of debility —	

Army Form C. 2118.

WAR DIARY
or
INTELLIGENCE SUMMARY
(Erase heading not required.)

Instructions regarding War Diaries and Intelligence Summaries are contained in F. S. Regs., Part II. and the Staff Manual respectively. Title Pages will be prepared in manuscript.

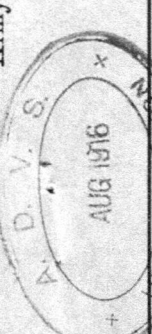

Place	Date	Hour	Summary of Events and Information	Remarks and references to Appendices
BAILLEUL	3/8/16	a.m.	Ro: See STAC – Condition of animals good – great improvement since my last inspection at VARENNIES.	
		p.m.	Went to inspect Farm at T.30 A.O.2 which I was instructed by D.D. had to be disinfected owing to mange when occupied by the 11th D.T.S. Carried out the disinfection – Reported b/s accordingly. Received wire from "Q" to disinfect standings at T.20 d.1.9 – Ordered Vet. 172nd Bde R Superior disinfection orgd. at T.	
	4/8/16	a.m.	Inspected 59th Divnl Batty at their request of the O.C. an' H.A.G. – Evacuated 5 horses for Vety reasons – was asked to see B. General Benson O.C. 5th Corps Hy Artillery – He spoke to me about his HO with whom he was very dissatisfied. I said I would represent the matter to the A.D.V.S.	
		p.m.	Office – Conference of Vety Officers.	
	5/8/16	a.m.	Drove by Office to the opposite end of BAILLEUL and joined the ADVS his train there.	
		p.m.	Visited SH-Q. at MONT NOIR and inspected all draftees & attached horses	

WAR DIARY
or
INTELLIGENCE SUMMARY

Army Form C. 2118.

(Erase heading not required.)

Place	Date	Hour	Summary of Events and Information	Remarks and references to Appendices
BAILLEUL	6/8/16	a.m.	Inspected the 109th Inf: Brigade with the exception of the 109 Tr. M. G. Coy, with results as under :— 9'" R. Innis: Fus — Condition of animals good. Shoeing bad. The following faults in shoeing noted — (a) animals not shod up to date in several cases in need of shoeing (b) & leaving to leave the feet too long & not reduce to their normal proportions (c) Mules shod with shoes of wrong size (d) No shoeing book kept. to shew the date on which animals are shod. 10'" R. Innis Fus — Condition of animals good, & shoeing outstandingly ⎱ Do 11'" R. Innis Fus — ⎰ Do 14'" R. I. R. — Several conditions unsatisfactory. The animals have fallen off considerably in condition since my last inspection. Shoeing bad. The same faults but to more marked degree as noted above at (a) & (b). This is the only Battalion which has a shoeing book for officer's return	

WAR DIARY or INTELLIGENCE SUMMARY

Army Form C. 2118.

Place	Date	Hour	Summary of Events and Information	Remarks and references to Appendices
BAILLEUL	7/8/16	a.m.	Inspected several proposed sites for the M.V.S. In wards standings — saw nothing suitable — Inspected horses for evacuation at the M.V.S. Same have to.c. M.V.S. to proceed with horses by road to No 23 V.Hosp.	
		p.m.	Inspected No 2 Coy A.S.C. — Horses in very good condition — Paid particular attention to the shoeing having heard that it had been adversely criticised — Evidences of — satisfactory, excepting the attached horses of No 1 Coy — These latter were not shod to date, & there was marked evidence of slumping —	
	8/8/16	a.m.	Inspected No 3 Coy A.S.C. — Condition of horses very good — Shoeing satisfactory	
		p.m.	A.D.V.S. Called — went with him to see the S.O.C. Lt Col 16 R.IF re LIEUT SULLIVAN whom the G.O.C. had placed under arrest.	
	9/8/16	a.m.	Went to inspect and distribute 88 remounts at Railhead.	
		p.m.	Routine	

WAR DIARY
or
INTELLIGENCE SUMMARY

Army Form C. 2118.

A.D.V.S. AUG 1916 ULSTER DIVISION

Place	Date	Hour	Summary of Events and Information	Remarks and references to Appendices
BAILEUL	10/8/16	6 am	Inspected transport animals of 108 bef. Bde including 108 M.G. Coy. butt results no invir — H. Div. — General condition good — Shoeing Shoers satisfactory — mules for the most part with overgrown feet. 9" R. I. Fus — General condition Shoeing satisfactory. 11" R. I. R. — do do 12" R. I. R. — do do 13 R. I. R. — General condition fair — Shoeing satisfactory. 108ᵗ M.G. Coy — General condition good — Shoeing — general tendency to "Stumping up" or dumping the toes.	
		pm	Inspected hos. Coy A.S.C. — General condition very good. Shoeing — all feet almost without exception show marked evidence of dumping	
	11/8/16	6 am	Routine - office	
		pm	Conference of Vety Officers	

WAR DIARY
or
INTELLIGENCE SUMMARY

Army Form C. 2118.

A. D. V. S. AUG 1916 ULSTER DIVISION

Place	Date	Hour	Summary of Events and Information	Remarks and references to Appendices
BAILLEUL	12/8/16	a.m.	Attended a conference held by the D.D.V.S. in BAILLEUL – Inspected the following units with results as under –	
		p.m.	121st Field Coy R.E. – General condition and shoeing satisfactory	
			122 " " " – Condition of animals satisfactory – Shoeing not up to date	
			150 " " " – Condition of animals fair – too many in foot. Condition – Shoeing satisfactory	
			109 Div. G. Coy – Condition of animals good – Shoeing very bad – 50% require shoeing – The O.C. complained of only having one set of tools for 2 farriers –	
	13/8/16	a.m.	Inspected following units –	
			159 H. Batty – Condition of horses good – Ringworm very prevalent.	
			1/1 Wessex Hy Batty – Condition very good – no skin disease	
		p.m.	Routine	

2449 Wt. W14957/M90 750,000 1/16 J.B.C. & A. Forms/C.2118/12.

Army Form C. 2118.

WAR DIARY
or
INTELLIGENCE SUMMARY
(Erase heading not required.)

Place	Date	Hour	Summary of Events and Information	Remarks and references to Appendices
BAILLEUL	14/8/16	a.m.	Went to A.H.Q. & saw D.A.D.M.G. about several matters	
		p.m.	Routine — Inspected new site for Mo. V.S. at S3 d 6 4 — Could find no suitable [or] units standings	
	15/8/16	a.m.	Routine	
		p.m.		
	16/8/16		Left for BOULOGNE to look over some Base Vety Hospitals — CAPT T.A. MCCLINTOCK acted as A.D.V.S. during my absence	
	19/8/16		Returned to D.H.Q. — Telegram from the D.V.S. awaiting me offering me the post of O.C. No. 1 Convalescent Horse depot — Spoke on phone with the D.V.S. and accepted the Post.	
	20/8/16	a.m.	Routine - office - Inspected the M.V.S. — Resumed Vety duties returning to Mules & St. Paul to their own Brigades	
		p.m.	Visited H.Q. 109 [inf] Bde transport - mules said to be unsuitable for draught.	
	21/8/16	a.m.	Inspected B C Battys 154 Bde — Condition of horses fair. Encountered 8 cases of debility - from Routine office	

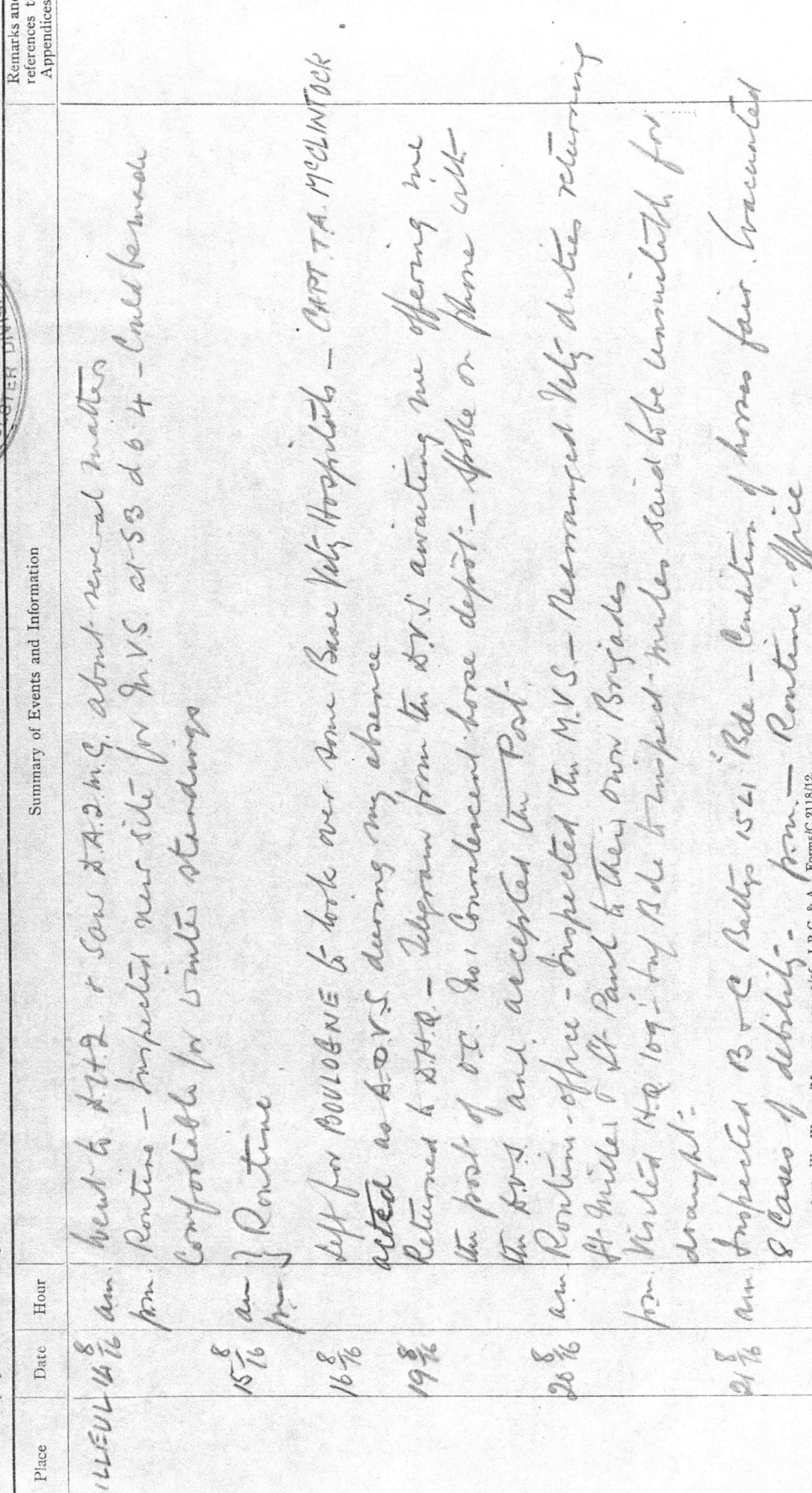

WAR DIARY or INTELLIGENCE SUMMARY

Army Form C. 2118.

A.D.V.S. AUG 1916 ULSTER DIVISION

Place	Date	Hour	Summary of Events and Information	Remarks and references to Appendices
BAILLEUL	22/8/16	a.m.	Inspected 13 Echelon S.A.C. – General condition very good – Have not pressed up as suddenly as might have been inspected since last inspection. p.m. Return – Office.	
	23/8/16	a.m.	Inspected the 4 public watering places – All but one to the future of running a right of the steps. Inspected Tanning huts – M.M.P. Condition of horses good – Stabling watering arrangements good. Detachment 36th Bde stationed by at WEST H OF FARM – Condition n ? – Good – several poor horses – hits dirty stalls outfits good. S.V. Collection – Condition of horses very good – Shoeing not up to date. p.m. Return – Office	
	24/8/16	a.m.	Return Div	

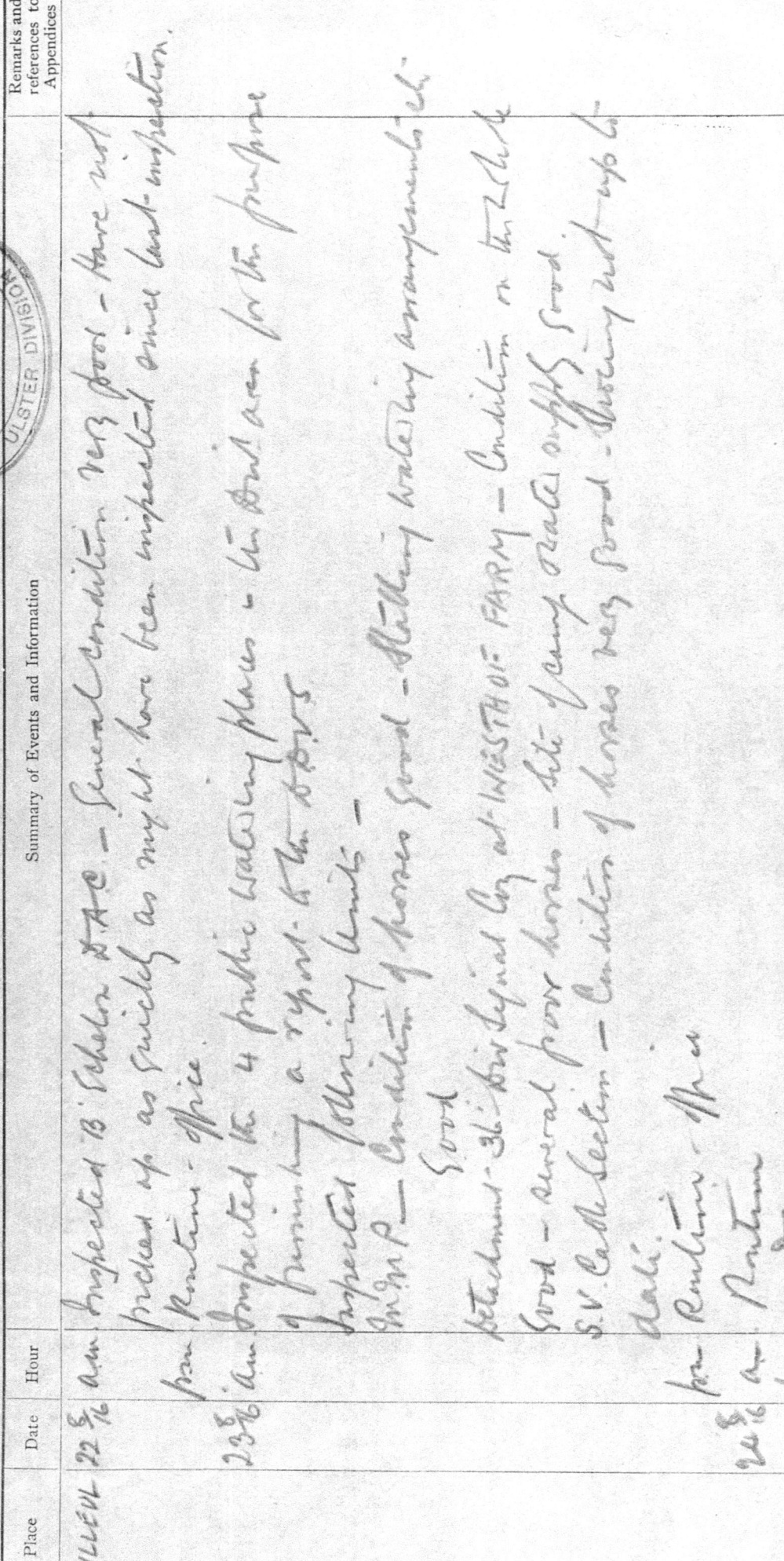

WAR DIARY
or
INTELLIGENCE SUMMARY

Army Form C. 2118.

A.D.V.S. AUG 1916 ULSTER DIVISION

Place	Date	Hour	Summary of Events and Information	Remarks and references to Appendices
Railleul	25/8/16	A.m.	Capt. T A McClintock acted as A.D.V.S. 36th Division. Major Webb leaving departed 9.30 a.m. Office Routine	
		P.m.	Routine	
	26/8/16	a.m.	Visited B.C & D Batteries 173 Bde R.F.A. Office Routine	
		P.m.	Visited Rel: Div Sup Coy. S.V. Case Sect- Thro M.P.	
	27/8/16	a.m.	Visited 16 R.A.R. & 167 R.B. Routine	
		P.m.	Visited A.Bty 173 R.F.A. & 30 R.B.	
	28/8/16	a.m.	Visited B C & D Btys R.F.A. Routine. R.J. wire to meet D.D.R. from 36 Div. w Surplus horses in A.S.C.	
		P.m.	Routine	
	29/8/16	a.m.	Visited horse standings mobile Troughs of A.S.C. & 173 Bde R.F.A. Met DDR at No 1 Coy A.S.C. with CO of A.S.C. inspected 1 Rider & 13 Heavy Draught. Took over 5th H Draught evacuated to M.V.S.	
		P.m.	Routine. Capt Horne A.V.C. arriving to take over duties of A.D.V.S. 36th Division. Reported arrival by wire to D.V.S. IVth Army.	
	30/8/16	a.m.	Reported in person to DAA & MG amst— other members of Div Staff. Reported Direct- Br Major R.A. Routine. D.D.V.S. 2nd Army called interviewing him & explaining delay in Joining 36 Div.	
		P.m.	Visited M.V.S. Routine. Road instructions for A.D.V.S. given in by D.D.V.S.	
	31/8/16	a.m.	Rox' nowy locating with Office Routine.	
		P.m.	Inspected M.V.S. Camp in good order turned found condition permanent standings in course of erection Inspected 10 cases of horses of "B" Echelon D.A.C. proceeding to Major I Du in connection with S.V. Saw the efficer C.R. N.Q. staff Office Routine.	A.D.V.S. Major I.D. A.W. Horne Major 31/8/16

WAR DIARY or INTELLIGENCE SUMMARY

Army Form C. 2118.

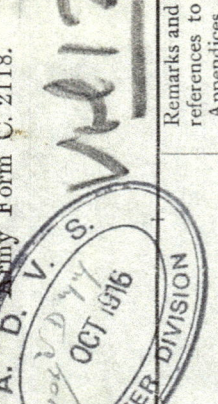
A.D.V.S. OCT 1916 ULSTER DIVISION

Place	Date	Hour	Summary of Events and Information	Remarks and references to Appendices
Bailleul	1.9.16	Am.	Inspected 108, 109 & 110 Field Ambulances. Horses in good condition. Will give expert few instructions on long feet, remarks on to O.C's. Three units were competing for tidy draught & dressings. Office Routine	
		Pm.	Inspected 16 pair of greys belongs to 36th Div Train began transport to Infantry Units. Condition Shoeing question from Divisors and IC O'Brand. Congress of ass VO's at 4 Pm. Office Routine.	
"	2.9.16	Am.	Inspected with Capt. Chown Div Sigual Coy RE Horses in good condition Shoeing good 7th Labour Battalion " " " very good " " Motorcal B Echelon DAC. 340 horses all majority in fair cond. About 30 in fair condition Office	
		Pm.	Working condition, not fat but well muscled up Shoeing good. M.G.D. Div. H.Q. An enquiry to begin arming Office Routine 7.30 Pm DHQS received interviews with Regt. Inspected horses of DHQ with Capt Chown.	
	3.9.16	Am.	Office Routine	
		Pm.	Office Routine	
	4.9.16	Am.	Office Routine. Inspected with Capt McClintock the following S.V. Cable Sect. good. Condition Shoeing fair C173 BDe Mostral condition good shoeing 13/43. Mostral condition WMP. good Condition shoeing fair No 1 Coy Div Train Shoeing good. A173 B RTA- Mostral condition Shoeing good. D173 B[?] Mg Coy Shoeing good. 1C RIR good condition 176 RB & 20 RB good condition. Wet Day	
		Pm	Interviewed Lt Morrison GVC. Office Routine Inspected Horses at MYS before evacuation	

WAR DIARY or INTELLIGENCE SUMMARY

Army Form C. 2118.

Place	Date	Hour	Summary of Events and Information	Remarks and references to Appendices
Bailleul	5.9.16	Am.	Met. Morning Office routine. read through OC's correspondence. Enclosures.	
		P.M	One case a horse of HQ 6r 153 Bde RFA sent to MVS as a mange suspect. diagnosed microscopically Positive Sarcoptic. VO/c immediately informed. by wire & orders to take all precautions & arrangements made to inspect tomorrow. Office routine very wet day.	
"	6.9.16	Am.	Fine day. Visited after Office HQ Gr 153 Bde RFA and Capt Shaw. gone into all particulars re mange case. Inspected HD Br Horses. good. 101st Inf Bde Animals. good. D Bty 153 Bde. Horses in fair condition. 108th Inf Bde. good. 12 RIR. MgCoy. 13 RIR 9/11 RIR very good. C Bty 153 Bde very good. A Bty 153 Bde good VO/c units reports tenesmus improvement arising last inspection by ADVS. Office routine reported mange case to DDVS & Staff	
	7.9.16	Am	Office routine inspected horses for evacuation at MVS	
		Pm	Routine	
	8.9.16	Am	Inspected with Capt Shaw MO1 Coy 36th Div Train Condition V.G. Shoeing improved good MO 4 " " " " MO 2 Sect DAC " " " "	
			Office	
		Pm	Conference of VO's Office Routine	

WAR DIARY
or
INTELLIGENCE SUMMARY

Army Form C. 2118.

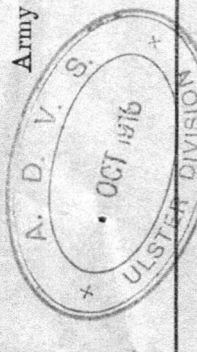
A.D.V.S. OCT 1916 ULSTER DIVISION

Place	Date	Hour	Summary of Events and Information	Remarks and references to Appendices
Bailleul	9/9/16	A.M.	Office Routine. Inspected with Capt Shaw A.V.C. 150th Field Coy R.E. Condition Fair. Shoeing good. Astore given re feeding etc. Shoeing good. 109th Infantry Brigade. 11 In Field good. 10 In Fld Fair. 14th Rifles Poor but V.O reports slight improvement. Shoeing improving. 9th R.I.F. good. Shoeing good.	
		P.M.	Office Routine. Talked to D.V.S. over Telephone re felp Medicines sent oversea with invent-Coy R.E.	
"	10/9/16	A.M.	Office Routine. Visited D.H.Q. Office Routine.	
		P.M.	Office Routine. Inspected DW Train at Rail Head in Bailleul.	
	11/9/16	A.M.	Office Routine. Inspected horses for evacuation at M.V.S. Office Routine.	
	12/9/16	A.M.	Office Routine. Interviewed St Miller went to D.H.Q. re organisation of Military.	
		P.M.	Office Routine.	
	13/9/16	A.M.	Office Routine. Interviewed St Morrison. Inspected horses at M.V.S. for evacuation.	
		P.M.	Office Routine.	
	14/9/16	A.M.	Inspected with Capt Chown. M.A.C. 4th Div. Army Workshop & Aust Tunneling Coy horses in good condition. Well shod. D.D.V.S. called.	
		P.M.	Arranged re distribution of V.O's duties. Office Routine.	

WAR DIARY
or
INTELLIGENCE SUMMARY
(Erase heading not required.)

Army Form C. 2118.

A.D.V.S. OCT 1916 ULSTER DIVISION

Place	Date	Hour	Summary of Events and Information	Remarks and references to Appendices
Ballard	15/9/16	am	Inspected No 3 Coy Div Train Horses. Very good condition. Faults in shoeing & pruning. Shoeing Cpng	
			121 " R&c " " " "	
			122 " R&c " " " moderate	
	pm	Office routine. Conference of VO's. Allotment of new unit explained.	
	16/9/16	am	Office Routine. Visited B branch re Clipping of horses. Selection of men for training as Cold Shoers & Inquiry Officers. Galloping their horses on the Roads	
	pm	Office routine	
	17/9/16	am	Inspected 119 Supplies horses at Berdulm. V.A.C. Inspected G & on "Wm Beck"	
			Weekly report to G. Office Routine	
	18/9/16	am	Office routine	
	pm	" "	
	19/9/16	am	Office routine. Brandy shoers at M.V.S. rode round to saw VO's at	
			Pranowlie.	
	pm	Went to Bu HQrs. Saw AA&QMG re Clipping Horses. Drove to Lurces & Cato to Artillery Horses	
	20/9/16	am	Office Routine. met DDR at B Echelon AC. Inspected the 102 horses of the reorganisation of Artillery DDR lost 37 & 62 cases for Surplus owing to reorganisation of Artillery - 1 Very weak sent to M.V.S. for evacuation - by Barge	
			evacuation. Delentis ; a Surprise green cases	
	pm	DDVS called. Inspected 5 horses at MVS. for proceeding en route for gt owen.	
			also arranged for 60 of the Delentis cases to proceed en route for gt owen	
			on morning of 21	

WAR DIARY
or
INTELLIGENCE SUMMARY

Army Form C. 2118.

Place	Date	Hour	Summary of Events and Information	Remarks and references to Appendices
Bailleul	21/9/16	Am	Office Routine. Inspected 174 B & RFA. A B/D Bailleul Horses in fair condition. Shoeing good. HQ Div very good.	
		Pm	DDVS called. Office routine.	
"	22/9/16	Am	Inspected with DDVS. 173 B.B. RFA. "B" "C" "D" Rady Horses "C" Rady of 18 Reserve cases. "B" Very Poor. 15 Beverley. A good rather sick 5 Debility. 150 Coy RE "B" Bty 153. B & RFA. 114 R.I.R. Improving 9th Ensu. Sur good. "B" Bty 153 B & good.	
		Pm	Conference of VO's DDVS present. Office routine.	
	23/9/16	Am	Hacked round saw VO's & some Units unofficially Office Routine	
		Pm	Office Routine	
	24/9/16	Am	Office Routine rendered weekly report to Q on Horses inspected during week.	
	25/9/16	Am	Office Routine. Inspected Horses at MVS before evacuation by Barge 9 not round enemy positions of Stationers	
		Pm	Road. Office Routine.	
	26/9/16	Am	Inspected with St. Morrison 71 87th Heavy Battery. Condition & Shoeing Poor. 110 th Heavy. Battery. Condition. Very good faults in Shoeing pointed out to O.C. 59 Seige B/y Horses. Shoeing good. No 2 Sec. 36 th D.A.C. Animals Shoeing good.	

WAR DIARY
or
INTELLIGENCE SUMMARY

(Erase heading not required.)

Army Form C. 2118.

Place	Date	Hour	Summary of Events and Information	Remarks and references to Appendices
Bailleul	26/9/16	PM	Office routine. D.D.V.S. called. Inspected M.V.S. Office routine	
"	27/9/16	AM	Inspected horses at M.V.S. then inspected with Lt Morrison 1/1 Heavy R.G.A. Brigade. H.Q. Bn R.G.A. IX Corps. 71st Heavy Battery R.G.A. Shoeing not 7 shoeing very good H.Q Siege R.H.A. & 30th up to date	
		PM	Office Routine	
	28/9/16	AM	Inspected No.3 & No.1 Coys Div. Train. Horses very good. Shoeing greatly improved	
		PM	Conference of V.O.'s. Routine.	
	29/9/16	AM	Office Routine. Went to M.V.S. Intervened Capt Wray & Inspected Cameron evening of 28/9/16 in absence of Capt Shaw A.V.C.	
		PM	Routine	
	30/9/16	AM	Attended Conference of D.D.V.S. & all A.D.V.S's 2 Army. Routine	
		PM	Routine	

C.S. Glover Major
A.D.V.S.
Ulster Division

10/1/16

Army Form C. 2118.

Vol 13

WAR DIARY
or
INTELLIGENCE SUMMARY
(Erase heading not required.)

Instructions regarding War Diaries and Intelligence Summaries are contained in F. S. Regs., Part II. and the Staff Manual respectively. Title Pages will be prepared in manuscript.

[Stamp: A.D.V.S. 3? YD 23? / NOV 1916 / ULSTER DIVISION]

Place	Date	Hour	Summary of Events and Information	Remarks and references to Appendices
Baiseulle	1.x.16	A.m.	Routine	
		P.m	A.D.V.S 16th Div came for Conference. Routine	
	2.x.16	A.m.	Inspected M.V.S. No 1 Sect. D.A.C. on dubbing care later evacuated. Horses on wire	
			in good condition, shoeing fair. Routine	
		P/m	Inspected No 2 Coy Div Train. Routine	
	3.x.16	A.m.	Routine. Interviewed Capt. Cluvon, Capt. Whyte & Lt. Morrison D.D.V.S. calling in	
			Special Sick Horse train. made necessary arrangements.	
		P.m	Routine. met D.D.V.S again & called on A.D.V.S 7th Div.	
	4.x.16	A.m.	Saw 200 horses off on Special Sick Horse Train. O.C. 48th M.V.S in charge.	
			Visited Q Branch of Staff then V.O/c 173 B? R.T.A.	
		P/m	Routine	
	5.x.16	A.M.	Inspected B Bty 153 Bde. D 173 B?. A 153 B?. C 173 B? & B 173 B?.	
			R.S. woke at M.V.S. for U.C away with Sick horse train 150 Coy R.E D 1049 2nd R?.	
		P.m	Office. Routine	
	6.x.16	A.M	Office Visited M.V.S. Inspected A Bty 173 B? R.F.A 150 Coy R.E D1049 2nd R?.	
		P.m	Office Conference of Y.O's.	

WAR DIARY
or
INTELLIGENCE SUMMARY

Army Form C. 2118.

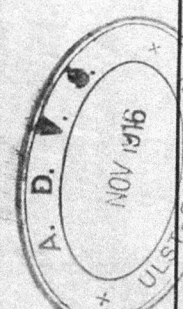

Place	Date	Hour	Summary of Events and Information	Remarks and references to Appendices
Bailleul	7.x.16	A.m.	Inspected "B" A & D Bdys R.F.A. 172 Brigade. Went into question of Forage Supply. Found Oats of poor quality & irregular receipt of equivalent for shortage of hay. Necessary steps taken. Small reports "A" Bdy no oatmeal in wagon line for 5 days. Horses very poor, & fallen off in condition. O.C. Brigade interviewed on this subject.	
		P.m.	Inspected 21 Remounts on arrival at Rail Hd. & Officer Routine.	
	8.x.16	A.m.	Office Routine.	
	9.x.16	A.m.	Routine	
		P.m.	Routine	
	10.x.16	A.m.	Interviewed Staff Capt. 36th Div. & Capt Wright A.V.C. inspected 109th Field Ambulance	
		P.m.	Visited Remount Depot at Caestre.	
	11.x.16	A.m.	Inspected 529 Howitzer Bdy. D Bdy 153 Bde. 121 Coy R.E. & C Bdy 153 B.de. Horses & Shoeing good. Office Routine.	
		P.m.	Inspected M.V.S. Office Routine.	
	12.x.16	A.m.	Inspected 108th Infantry Bde. Horses good. Shoeing much 9th Inniskillen Poor. Company going on in 13 R.I.R. Y.O. informed & all action taken to prevent recurrence. faulty Office routine	
		P.m.	Routine Office	

WAR DIARY
or
INTELLIGENCE SUMMARY
(Erase heading not required.)

Army Form C. 2118.

Place	Date	Hour	Summary of Events and Information	Remarks and references to Appendices
Bullest	15X16	Am	Inspected 107th Inyuskuy Penysh & 122 Coy R.E. Lt/ R.E. Evans were on the pur Sidr: & web gorery were driving goldones re dictric manyment given	
		Pm	Conference of T.O's. Rasion Officer.	
	16X16	Am	Office Inspected H.Qrs. 7B Echelon D.A.C. now one mules except 24 also 110 F Ambulance. Office	
		Pm	Routine.	
	15X16	Am	Office. Inspected M.M.P. S.V. Case Coy 8th But Bat. K.O.Th. Special 13rd Lt R.I.R. Pioneer 20 A.T.R.E. 2 Coys 11th Lab-Bat-B.C. 7th Lab Bat Coy. motored to Belendniguse though 3 section of line called on D.D.V.S.	
Routine	(15X16	Am		
		Pm		
	17X16	Am	Inspected 529 Bty R.F.A. (C172) 9 own aminals after Mallein Tepl. Inspected 173 But R.F.A. & interviewed 90/Sergt. 2 vans A.V.C. also Lt D113.	
		Pm	Routine.	
	18X16	Am	Inspected 903 Coy A.S.C. & M.V.S.	
		Pm	Lecture to A/Sergts A.V.C. 5 NCO's absent Staff Capt R.A. unable accordingly Routine.	

WAR DIARY or **INTELLIGENCE SUMMARY**
(Erase heading not required.)

Army Form C. 2118.

Place	Date	Hour	Summary of Events and Information	Remarks and references to Appendices
Bailleul	19.XI.16	a.m.	Interview with DDVS 2 Army B Bty 153 B⁺. D.173 B⁺. A153 C173 B 173. 9 C 112 Capt McClintock returning from leave.	
		P.M.	Routine.	
"	20.XI.16	a.m.	Routine	
		P.M.	Yielded advance Remount Sect. Congener of VO's routine	
	21.XI.16	a.m.	Routine	
		P.M.	Routine interviewed OC of "B" 173 B⁺. re fellingtin Brown gut.	
	22.XI.16	a.m.	Routine. Sent weekly report to S. Returns	
		P.M.	Routine.	
	23.X.16	A.M.	Routine. 46 Remount Casualties inspected & dealt with. G.D.V.S. proceeded on leave duties performed while absent by D.C.M.V.S.	
		P.M.	Office routine	
	24.XI.16	A.M.	Routine report to DOVS re French horse found by A Bty/173 Bde RFA	
		P.M.	Office routine.	
	25.XI.16	A.M.	Routine	
		P.M.	Office routine D.O.V.S. called at office	

Army Form C. 2118.

WAR DIARY
or
INTELLIGENCE SUMMARY
(Erase heading not required.)

A. D. V. S.
NOV 1916
ULSTER DIVISION

Place	Date	Hour	Summary of Events and Information	Remarks and references to Appendices
BAILLEUL	26.x.16	A.M.	Routine	
		P.M.	Office Routine. D.D.V.S. called at Office	
	27.x.16	A.M.	Routine	
		P.M.	Office Routine. Conference of Vety officers.	
	28.x.16	A.M.	Routine	
		P.M.	Office Routine	
	29.x.16	A.M.	Routine	
		P.M.	Office Routine	
	30.x.16	A.M.	Routine	
		P.M.	Office Routine	
	31.x.16	A.M.	Routine	
	31.x.16	P.M.	Routine	

A S Glamor Major AVC
A.D.V.S. 36 Ulster Division 2/c.

Army Form C. 2118.

WAR DIARY
or
INTELLIGENCE SUMMARY

(Erase heading not required.)

Instructions regarding War Diaries and Intelligence Summaries are contained in F. S. Regs., Part II. and the Staff Manual respectively. Title Pages will be prepared in manuscript.

Original Vol 14

ULSTER DIVISION — A.D.V.S. 30 NOV 1916

Place	Date	Hour	Summary of Events and Information	Remarks and references to Appendices
BAILLEUL	1/11/16	Am	Routine	
		Pm	Routine	
	2/11/16	Am	Routine	
		Pm	A.D.V.S. Maj Horner returned from leave of absence. Reported his arrival	
	3/11/16	Am	Office Routine interviewed Capt Chown who had acted during my absence went through all correspondence orders etc accumulated during my absence.	
		Pm	Routine Conference of V.O's.	
	4/11/16	Am	Routine Inspected 172 B & R.T.A interviewed Capt Paul.	
		Pm	Routine	
	5/11/16	Am	Visited "Q" re giving lectures and horses back 10.30 Office	
		Pm	Routine	
	6/11/16	Am	Interviewed Capt Chown re lectures etc Routine	
		Pm	Inspected M.V.S. Dyoung work progressing well & satisfactory. Routine	
	7/11/16	Am	Routine Very wet	
		Pm	Routine	
	8/11/16	Am	Inspected No 2 Sect D.A.C. A Bty 173 C Bty 172 B Bty 153 D 173 A 153.	
		Pm	Routine	

WAR DIARY
or
INTELLIGENCE SUMMARY
(Erase heading not required.)

Army Form C. 2118.

A.D.V.S.
NOV 1916
ULSTER DIVISION

Place	Date	Hour	Summary of Events and Information	Remarks and references to Appendices
Ballent	9/11/16	am	Inspected C 173 Bt. B 173 Bt. 150 R.E. No 3 Sect. D.A.C. Nos 2-3 Bts	
		pm	Coys A.S.C.	
		pm	Routine	
	10/16	am	Saw 9.O.C's charge 107 Bt in consolidation readily Remount Report called	
		pm	On D.V.S. discussed Jananys Vety Lectures	
		pm	Conference	
	11/11/16	am	Inspected D. Bt/153 Bt. 121 Coy R.E. 20th Army Troops R.E. No 1 Sect DAC	
		pm	Routine	
	12/11/16	am	Inspected No 1 Coy A.S.C.	
		pm	Went to Remount with Bt. General Middlecombs selected him 2 charges to replace those lost by shell fire	
	13/11/16	am	Inspected all Div HQ animals & consulted re lectures & arranged for	
			Div Orders re shoeing with Tin.	
		pm	Pm Routine - Vety Lecture 5-30 to 6-45	
	14/11/16	am	Visits with D.A.D.O.S. Remount Report to select two horses. Routine	
		pm	Routine Vety Lecture 5-30 to 6-45.	
	15/11/16	am	Inspected with V.O./c 107th Infantry Bgr. Routine	
		pm	Routine	

WAR DIARY or INTELLIGENCE SUMMARY

Army Form C. 2118.

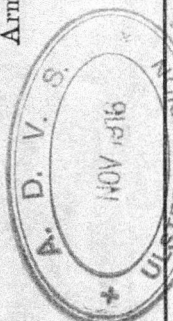

Place	Date	Hour	Summary of Events and Information	Remarks and references to Appendices
Pauluel	16/11/16	am	Routine visited A. Branch	
		pm	Routine Inspected at M.V.S. horses for evacuation Routine grantomes Office	
	17/11/16	am	Visited Riv. HQ Arr. Routine	
		pm	Routine Conference of M.O's	
	18/11/16	am	Routine visited Dentist	
		pm	Routine	
	19/11/16	am	Routine visited Dentist	
		pm	Routine	
	20/11/16	am	Visited A. Routine	
		pm	Practice Demonstration at M.V.S. G.O.C. called at M.V.S. to see his method of shoeing with the epsom return	
	21/11/16	am	Inspected animals of No 2 Sect D.A.C.	
		pm	Visited Dentist Routine	
	22/11/16	am	Routine Inspected . 109 Field Ambulance B Echelon D.A.C. TH.3 Bn D.A.C.	
		pm	Routine	
	23/11/16	am	Routine inspected gunfire Heavy Bde at 153 Bde RFA	
		pm	DDVS called Inspected with him 130 Heavy Bde & 113th Heavy Bde Corps Troops	

WAR DIARY
INTELLIGENCE SUMMARY

Army Form C. 2118.

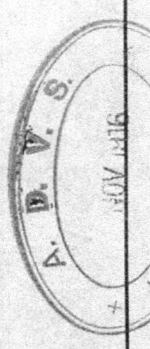

Place	Date	Hour	Summary of Events and Information	Remarks and references to Appendices
Ballut	24/11/16	AM	Inspected 109th Infantry Bde.	
		PM	Routine. Vety Conference. Visited M.V.S. to examine Skin Scrapings	
	25/11/16	AM	Telephoned DDVS re suspected Mange in No 2 Sect-DAC. Arranged for him to come & see the animals at 2.30 PM. Inspected M.M.P. & 108th Infantry Bgde	
		PM	DDVS called at Office. Inspected M.V.S. Unit supposed Sarcoptic Parasite. After the Mules of DAC. from which the Parasite was taken & declared it not to be Mange. Routine.	
	26/11/16	AM	Routine. Rendering weekly report to Q. Report on showing 10TDDVS.	
		PM	Visited M.V.S. Routine.	
	27/11/16	AM	Routine	
		PM	Routine	
	28/11/16	AM	Inst. 39 Remounts at Rail Head inspected & du Intuitig Same	
		PM	Inspected Surplus horses of R.E. & undergoing Unit.	
	29/11/16	AM	Routine	
		PM	Routine Examination Mules to A.V.C Surgerie after six weeks course of instruction	
	30/11/16	AM	Routine inspected No 2 D.A.C.	
		PM	Routine	

A.L. Turner Major
AVS 36 Division
30.11.16

WAR DIARY
or
INTELLIGENCE SUMMARY

Army Form C. 2118.

Place	Date	Hour	Summary of Events and Information	Remarks and references to Appendices
BAILLEUL	1/12/16	A.M	Inspected Remount Cases for Casting also 122 Coy R.E. 16 R.I.R. Purveyors	
		P.M	9/10 Field Ambulance Routine	
	2/12/16	A.M	Vety Conference Routine	
		P.M	Inspected 20 A.T. Coy Routine	
	3/12/16	A.M	Routine	
		P.M	Routine Visited Q Branch	
	4/12/16	A.M	Inspected "B" 153 B. D 173 B. Q 153 B. & C 173 B.	
		P.M	Routine Interviewed Capt. McClintock re skin cases in Battalion at C.173.	
	5/12/16	A.M	Visited M.V.S. Inspected 2nd Army Workshops.	
		P.M	Routine	
	6/12/16	A.M	Inspected "B" 173 No 3 Sect D.A.C. C 172 A 173	
		P.M	Lecture to A.V.C. Scuff.	
	7/12/16	A.M	Parade for Casting Vet. Cases. Routine	
		P.M	Routine	
	8/12/16	A.M	Met Remounts 24 at Rail Head.	
		P.M	Congratre 6 V.O's taken by O.C. M.V.S. as ANVS was sick.	

Army Form C. 2118.

WAR DIARY
or
INTELLIGENCE SUMMARY

(Erase heading not required.)

Instructions regarding War Diaries and Intelligence Summaries are contained in F.S. Regs., Part II. and the Staff Manual respectively. Title Pages will be prepared in manuscript.

Place	Date	Hour	Summary of Events and Information	Remarks and references to Appendices
Boulful	9/12/16	Am	Routine. ADVS "Sick"	
		PM		
	10/12/16	Am	Routine " " DDVS called in afternoon	
		PM		
	11/12/16	Am	Routine Sent report to Q	
		PM	Routine	
	12/12/16	AM	Routine. ADVS admitted to hospital duties taken on by O.C. M.V.S	
		PM	Routine D.D.V.S. called in afternoon	
	13/12/16	AM	Routine inspect Horse dip at St Jan CAPPEL	
		PM	Routine	
	14/12/16	AM	Routine	
		PM	Routine	
	15/12/16	A.M.	Routine inst. HORSE DIP. with D.D.V.S. Report to "Q" re Shrews	
		PM	Routine Conference of V.Os	
	16/12/16	AM	Routine	
		P.M.	Routine	

Army Form C. 2118.

WAR DIARY
or
INTELLIGENCE SUMMARY

(Erase heading not required.)

Instructions regarding War Diaries and Intelligence Summaries are contained in F.S. Regs., Part II. and the Staff Manual respectively. Title Pages will be prepared in manuscript.

A.D.V.S.
JAN 1917
ULSTER DIVISION

Place	Date	Hour	Summary of Events and Information	Remarks and references to Appendices
Bailleul	17/12/16	A.M.	Routine	
		P.M.	Routine	
	18/12/16	A.M.	Routine. Visit "Horse dip" at St Jans Cappel.	
		P.M.	Routine	
	19/12/16	A.M.	Routine	
		P.M.	Routine	
	20/12/16	A.M.	Routine. Case of mange in 14 R.I.R. unit inspected & cases animals finally examined. Case reported to A.D.V.S.	
		P.M.	Routine	SM REOPTIC
	21/12/16	A.M.	Routine. Visit & inspect dip at St Jans Cappel	
		P.M.	Routine	
	22/12/16	A.M.	Routine. 2nd full report on mange in 14 R.I.R. to A.D.V.S.	
		P.M.	Routine. Conference of V.O.s	
	23/12/16	A.M.	Routine	
		P.M.	Routine	
	24/12/16	A.M.	Routine. A.D.V.S. returning to Derry from Hospital reporting Summa.	
		P.M.		

WAR DIARY or INTELLIGENCE SUMMARY

Army Form C. 2118.

Place	Date	Hour	Summary of Events and Information	Remarks and references to Appendices
25/12/16		am	Routine	
		Pm	Routine	
26/12/16		am	Routine	
		Pm	Routine	
	27/12/16	am	Routine	
		Pm	Routine	
	28/12/16	am	Inspected with Lt. Morrison some office Corps Heavy Artillery	
			130 Bdy.	
		Pm	Visited ADVS 2nd Army for consultation	
	29/12/16	am	Routine. Capt McClintock proceeded on the march with RFA.	
		Pm	Routine. Vety Conference.	
	30/12/16	am	Office Routine. Inspected B172 & D172 RFA.	
		Pm	Inspected ID153 RFA.	
	31/12/16	am	Sgt- Bailleul with OC DivTrain to RFA Training Area Inspected 173 Bde RFA on the march. Stays night at Bonbergue.	

A. S. Turner Major
ADVS 36th Division
Trees 1·1·17.

Army Form C. 2118.

WAR DIARY
or
INTELLIGENCE SUMMARY
(Erase heading not required.)

Instructions regarding War Diaries and Intelligence Summaries are contained in F. S. Regs., Part II. and the Staff Manual respectively. Title Pages will be prepared in manuscript.

Place	Date	Hour	Summary of Events and Information	Remarks and references to Appendices
Bailleul	1/1/17	am	Left Boulogne & returned to Bailleul arriving Bailleul 7.15 P.m.	
	2/1/17	am	Routine	
		Pm	Inspected with Brigade Commander A B9D Batteries R.F.A.	
	3/1/17	am	Routine	
		Pm	Inspected Horse Ry. at St Jean Capel. visited M.V.S. to examine	
			Skin Scraping at 3 Sec. D.A.C. Routine	
	4/1/17	am	Inspected No 3 Sec. D.A.C. 59 Siege Battery. D171 1" Heavy Battery	
		Pm	Inspected Horse Caws at M.V.S. routine	
	5/1/17	am	Inspected B. 153 Bde. A 153 Bde. C 173 Bde. & C 172 Bde.	
		Pm	Routine. O.O's Conference.	
	6/1/17	am	Inspected No 2 Sec. D.A.C. met DDVS & French Officer at Corps Horse Ry.	
		Pm	Routine.	
	7/1/17	am & Pm	Visited Artillery Bde at Training Area. Visited Brown Capt McClintock to arrange in Vety Charge.	
	8/1/17	am	Routine. Sent reports to DDVS & B re B Pety 173 Bde.	
		Pm	Routine.	

WAR DIARY or INTELLIGENCE SUMMARY

Army Form C. 2118.

Place	Date	Hour	Summary of Events and Information	Remarks and references to Appendices
Bailleul	9/1/17	am	Inspected "C" Sub 173 Bde Ammunition Coln. Staff Capt R.A. Saw Major Lowe Intelligence officer 147 Heavy Bgde in connection of "B" 173 Bde of Edinburgh. Also O.C. No. 3 Sub DAC in watering trough difficulties. HQ offrs & others interviewed with A.A. D.V.S. re mange	DDVS 2 Army
		Pm	Called 4.30 Pm	
	10/1/17	am	Inspected C172 No 2 Sub DAC B153 Re mange. Very Conspicuous	
		Pm	Conference completing routine	
	11/1/17	am	Inspected A 153 Routine	
		Pm	Inspected with DDVS C173 & 147 H.A. Veterinary Lecture Routine	
	12/1/17	am	Interviewed IX Corps. Arranged for lorry to set mange from office of DDVS & 2nd Army. To be ready at an hours notice after Jan 15.	
			Non permanent fatigue party to be ready at an hours notice	
			Inspected No 1 Sub DAC 100 Empt Mange Cases. Routine	
	13/1/17	am	Routine Very Conference Veterinary Lecture	
		Pm	Inspected B 142 D 153 & A 142	
	14/1/17	am	Routine Lecture	
		Pm	Routine	
	15/1/17	am	Inspected all horses for evacuation at No V.S. Inspected 19 to Echelon DAC	
		Pm	Practice Lecture at No V.S. DDVS called round Home Rep Rouen	

WAR DIARY or INTELLIGENCE SUMMARY

Army Form C. 2118.

Place	Date	Hour	Summary of Events and Information	Remarks and references to Appendices
Bailleul	16/1/17	Am	Routine. Inspected A & D Batteries 173rd Bde	
		PM	Inspected No 3 Sect. D.A.C. & some horse standings belonging to No 2 Sect. D.A.C. from no sid. Telephoned Staff Capt R.A. with regard to this transport. Office Routine.	
	17/1/17	Am	Conference of A.D.V.S's with D.D.V.S 2nd Army. Visited Horse Dep.	
		PM	Conference of V.O's.	
			Routine. Conference IX Corps	
	18/1/17	Am	Inspected C 153. Arranged for Sawyer Stove, Blue lamps etc	
		PM	Routine	
	19/1/17	Am	Inspected 108 Infy Bde 121st R.E.	
		PM	16 R.I.R. Pioneers. Vety Conference Routine.	
	20/1/17	Am	Inspected 108 & 109 Infy Brigades	
		PM	"D" 172, 122 R.S, HQ. Qu 172 R.F.A. HQ Qu 107 Infy Bde. Routine	
	21/1/17	Day	Met D.D.V.S at IX Corps Horse Dep. Called on Capt & SSO & DADOS IX Corps Arranged with AAQ Mg on telephone for ASC to supply men for disinfecting.	
		PM	Routine.	

WAR DIARY or INTELLIGENCE SUMMARY

Army Form C. 2118.

A.D.V.S.
JAN 1917
ULSTER DIVISION

Place	Date	Hour	Summary of Events and Information	Remarks and references to Appendices
Belfast	22/1/17	Am	Inspected 36th Div Signal Coy Head Qrs.	
		Pm	MVS also many cases 32 per week also 108th Field Ambulance	
			109th F.A. Routine.	
	23/1/17	Am	Inspected 36th Div Train	
		Pm	" " "	Routine.
	24/1/17	Am	Inspected 107th M.G. Coy. 36th Motor Bar. 8th Entrenching Bat. M.M.P. 150 Coy R.E.	
		Pm	110th Field Ambulance. 2nd Army Workshops. K. Coy Cases Section Routine.	
	25/1/17	Am	Inspected at Rep interviewed OO, PSO IX Corps also IX Corps Q. n Horse Rep	
		Pm	Conference with OC MVS n Horse Rep all arrangements ready for move when ordered. Interviewed Q.A. Q.M.G. IX Corps.	
	26/1/17	Am	Visited Rep with CE IX Corps interviewed Q.A. Q.M.G. 36th Div re detailing units for Rep. Failure badly to arrive- MVS Sandary Section Tramway D.1533 re Road sheep in washing for Rep- Interviewed IX Corps Q. re Short here etc	
		Pm	Holy Communion Routine. Interviewed Q.A. Q.M.G. IX Corps.	
	27/1/17	Am	Rehearsal at IX Corps Horse Rep. DADQMG IX Corps observes 2nd Army present- Horses O, 48 MVS dipped	
		Pm	Visited IX Corps Routine.	

Army Form C. 2118.

WAR DIARY
or
INTELLIGENCE SUMMARY
(Erase heading not required.)

Instructions regarding War Diaries and Intelligence Summaries are contained in F.S. Regs., Part II. and the Staff Manual respectively. Title Pages will be prepared in manuscript.

Place	Date	Hour	Summary of Events and Information	Remarks and references to Appendices
Present Boulleuil	28/1/17	AM PM	7.30 to 12.30 at IX Corps Horse Dpt. "B" 153 Dipping Routine	
	29/17	AM PM	Visited Horse Dpt. E.O.C. 36th Div called in. Saw animals of No 2 Sect. DAC Inspected A 173 horses which are being Issued 2 platoons of Dpt. to ADVS 15th Division visited Corps re allotting Train to 41 & 23 Divs at request of DDVS. Routine Visited at Dpt. Routine	
	30/17	AM PM	Appearing to OC 48 MVS rendered for arrs. Routine	
	31/17	AM PM	Routine Repaired 11 AM on leave Spence Major Privat appears Capt. Craven took on duties of ADVS 36th Div temporarily	

Jan 31st 1917.

A. S. Glover. Major.
ADVS 36th Division

Army Form C. 2118.

WAR DIARY
or
INTELLIGENCE SUMMARY
(Erase heading not required.)

Instructions regarding War Diaries and Intelligence Summaries are contained in F.S. Regs., Part II. and the Staff Manual respectively. Title Pages will be prepared in manuscript.

Place	Date	Hour	Summary of Events and Information	Remarks and references to Appendices
Bailleul	1/2/17	A.M.	Routine. In attendance IX Corps. Horse. D.I.P. from 10AM to 4 PM.	
		P.M.	Routine.	
	2/2/17	A.M.	Routine. 1 case ulcerative cellulitis reported from C 173 Bde RFA same reported D.D.V.S. 2nd ARMY.	
		P.M.	Routine. Conference of V.Os. D.D.V.S. 2nd ARMY. Calls at office.	
	3/2/17	A.M.	Routine. Inspected B 153 Bde RFA, D 173 Bde RFA & C 173 Bde RFA with D.D.V.S.	
		P.M.	Routine. arrange work "Q" 36 Div" for construction of disinfecting shed at M.V.S.	
	4/2/17	A.M.	Routine. Present at cleaning of IX Corps Horse D.I.P.	
		P.M.	Routine. Conference of V.Os.	
	5/2/17	A.M.	Routine.	
		P.M.	Routine.	
	6/2/17	A.M.	Routine. Inspected 130 Heavy Battery with V.O. Send report to D.D.V.S. on same	
		P.M.	Routine. Attend IX Corps. Horse D.I.P.	

Army Form C. 2118.

WAR DIARY
or
INTELLIGENCE SUMMARY
(Erase heading not required.)

Instructions regarding War Diaries and Intelligence Summaries are contained in F. S. Regs., Part II. and the Staff Manual respectively. Title Pages will be prepared in manuscript.

A.D.V.S. FEB 1917 ULSTER DIVISION

Place	Date	Hour	Summary of Events and Information	Remarks and references to Appendices
Bailleul	7/2/17	A.M.	Routine	
		P.M.	Routine. Lecture to N.C. Sergeants on treatment of mange	
	8/2/17	A.M.	Routine	
		P.M.	Routine	
	9/2/17	A.M.	Routine. Jane over, examine & distribute 31 Remounts. 10 Vehyds. Cars mange found same reported SDVS & "Q" 36 Bn.	
		P.M.	Routine. Conference of V.Os. ADVS 16th Inf. Called at office. About 14 Corps. D.I.P.	
	10/2/17	A.M.	Routine. Visit & inspect A & B Batty 172 Bde RFA.	
		P.M.	Routine.	
	11/2/17	A.M.	Routine. Visit & inspect 2nd Bazan Corps HQrs.	
		P.M.	Routine. ADVS 16th Inf. called.	
	12/2/17	A.M.	Routine. Visit 14 Corps. D.I.P.	
		P.M.	Routine.	
	13/2/17	A.M.	Routine.	
		P.M.	Routine. Inspect with D.D.V.S. 2nd Army, 130 Heavy Batty, & A & B Batty 172 Bde R.F.A. DDVS took mobile section & inspect champ-dog Shed.	

WAR DIARY or INTELLIGENCE SUMMARY

Army Form C. 2118.

A.D.V.S. FEB 1917 ULSTER DIVISION

Place	Date	Hour	Summary of Events and Information	Remarks and references to Appendices
BAILLEUL	14/2/17	A.M.	Routine. Visit 14 Corps. D.I.P.	
		P.M.	Routine. ADVS 16 Divn Calls.	
	15/2/17	A.M.	Routine. attend demonstration on "Mange" by Capt hick Pillers 23 Vety Hospital	
		P.M.	with Capts McClintock, Conochie, Millar Tosky &	
	16/2/17	A.M.	Routine. visit 14 Corps O/c	
		P.M.	Routine. Enquiries of V.D.s	
	17/2/17	A.M.	Routine. Shoeing Schemes comes into force.	
		P.M.	Routine. Visit 14 Corps. D.I.P.	
	18/2/17	A.M.	Routine. Visit 14 Corps 'Q' & branches for HORSE DIP	
		P.M.	Routine. Office	
	19/2/17	A.M.	Routine. Visit 14 Corps D.I.P. 3 cases Stomatitis Contagiosa reported by OC 23 Vet Hosp in C/173 RFA, 11 RIR, Interviewed Capt. MILLAR AVC	
		P.M.	Routine. Report BDDVS on STOMATITIS. visit DHQ & Mange	
	20/2/17	A.M.	Routine. Visit 14 Corps DIP. A & B Batty 172 RFA & 121 RE through dip. Visit DHQ & Mange	
		P.M.	Routine. Visit & inspect 130 Heavy Batty & 71 Heavy Batty hill V.O. Interviewed Capt McCulloch MC further report 6 cases of "D" 16 & 17 in Stratzeele.	

Army Form C. 2118.

WAR DIARY
or
INTELLIGENCE SUMMARY
(Erase heading not required.)

A.D.V.S.
FEB 1917
ULSTER DIVISION

Place	Date	Hour	Summary of Events and Information	Remarks and references to Appendices
BAILLEUL	21/2/17	AM	Routine attend Cdp with 14 Corps "Q"	
		P.M.	Routine. Have a D.O. published on STOMATITIS, CONTAGIOSA.	
	22/2/17	AM	Routine. Take over administration of 113 ARMY. F.A. Bde. y/c CAPT FARROL A.V.C.	
		PM	Routine. interviews Capt WO CONOCHIE. called on A.D.V.S. 25 Bn.	
	23/2/17	A.M.	Routine. Inspect 2nd ANZAC CORPS HQRS	
		P.M.	Routine. Conference of V.D.s A.D.V.S. 16 Div. Calls v visit mobile section	
	24/2/17	AM	Routine. Jans now examine & chotulali 62 Remounts to units of 36 Div, DDVS calls at 9/pu	
			& visit mobile section. inspect 130 Heavy Batty R.G.A. evacuate 13 cases for debility, 400 cases mange	
		P.M.	Routine. Visit v inspect. 130 Heavy Batty R.G.A.	
			reported as cured to D.D.V.S.	
	25/2/17	AM	Routine	
		PM	Major Horne returned for duty from Special Leave & Sick List	
	26/2/17	AM	Inspected 173 Bde R.F.A.	
		Pm	Routine. DDVS called 7.30 P.m.	
	27/2/17	Am	Inspected animals at 108th Army Bde. S.R. & D153rd R.A.S evacuated 9	
		PM	Inspected surplus animals at B Echelon horses. re disposal Routine.	
	28/2/17 Am		Inspected B.A.C. 113 Bde Army R.F.A. A Bty 113 Bde.	
		Pm	Routine. Vety conference	2 28/2/17

A.S.Jones Major ADVS
36th Division

WAR DIARY or INTELLIGENCE SUMMARY

Army Form C. 2118.

A.D.V.S. 31/VD407 MAR 1917 ULSTER DIVISION

V6/1

Place	Date	Hour	Summary of Events and Information	Remarks and references to Appendices
BAILLEUL	1/3/17	Am	Inspected HQrs & D Bty, 113 Army Bde RFA. Inspected No.1 Sec DAC	
		Pm	Routine. Visited Corps Q.	
	2/3/17	Am	Visited Dep. Div HQrs. Inspected 2 yr old colts - eight by Canadians 1914.	
		Pm	Inspected 22 Supply lorries at Prowreous linen Drum Supply Bde.	
			Routine. Visited Corps Q & drew up weekly programme for Dep.	
			Vety Congress.	
	3/3/17	Am	Met DDVS 2nd Army 10.30 am Inspected with him 113 Bde Ammn Column Q	
			A Bty 113 Bde	
		Pm	Visited Horse Bredin Frigh Dep with DDVS. Routine. visited IX Corps Q.	
			Blankets at veni Dep. Routine	
	4/3/17	Am	Inspected 130 Heavy Bty with Lieut Morrison	
		Pm	Routine	
	5/3/17	Am	Routine inspected B Echelon DAC HQ & DAC Pk MYS	
		Pm	Routine visited OO IX Corps Q & IX Corps Q. re Horse Dep Blankets.	
	6/3/17	Am	Routine. Inspected horses at MYS previous to evacuation. Visited Horse Dep @ 2.30 Pm	
		Pm	Inspected No 2 Sect DAC with OC.	
			& C'2 IX Corps	
	7/3/17	Am	Inspected 14th R.I.R. 9th Inn Fus. 11th R.I.F. 10th R.I.F. 122 Coy R.E. Interviewed	
			Capt Carmichael a/c Chauffeurs. Arranged Veterinary Officer	
		Pm	Routine visited IX Corps Q & saw Coe Morlière	

Army Form C. 2118.

WAR DIARY
or
INTELLIGENCE SUMMARY
(Erase heading not required.)

Instructions regarding War Diaries and Intelligence Summaries are contained in F.S. Regs., Part II. and the Staff Manual respectively. Title Pages will be prepared in manuscript.

A. D. V. S.
MAR 1917
ULSTER DIVISION

Place	Date	Hour	Summary of Events and Information	Remarks and references to Appendices
Raillencourt	8/3/17	Am	Routine. Visited M.V.S. Saw Cpl M's Change. Visited 17 Corps Horse Dep. Visited Q 36 Res'n. Routine.	
		Pm	Visited Corps Q & Col Maddens Group. Routine.	
	9/3/17	Am	Capt Brown O.C. 48 M.V.S. proceeded on leave. Later over by British Visited M.V.S. Inspected D 15'b B9. Routine.	
		Pm	Conference of V.O's 4 to 5.30 P.m. Routine.	
	10/3/17	Am	Visited M.V.S. did work there. 17 Corps Horse Dep arranged troops inspected.	
		Pm	Pro Serg. Cpl. H.Q. Div called on Q.B.A. re move. Inspected 14 animals at M.V.S. for return to Remounts. Inspected horses at 108 & 109 Field Ambulances. Routine.	
	11/3/17	Am	Routine. Arranged units for Dep. Returns. Reports. Inspected horses at 2nd Anzac H.Q. Div.	
		Pm	Routine.	
	12/3/17	Am	Visited M.V.S. had men inspecting their visited Dep.	
		Pm	At Dep from 1.30 till 5 P.m awaiting mal- from D.V.S. Routine.	
	13/3/17	Am	Routine. Inspected horses at M.V.S. began learning for Bays. Inspected D 16 B9.	
		Pm	A 17/3 saw certificate for Cmdr Oats for 26 animals A/13. Visited Q 36 Res.	
	14/3/17	Am	Visited Horse Dep inspected at Sy Cay. B Div. H.Q. Div visited Q.	
		Pm	Visited 17 Corps Q. Routine. Visited OO 17 Corps & SOR 2.	

WAR DIARY or INTELLIGENCE SUMMARY

Army Form C. 2118.

(Erase heading not required.)

A.D.V.S.
MAR 1917
ULSTER DIVISION

Place	Date	Hour	Summary of Events and Information	Remarks and references to Appendices
Belfast	15.3.17	am	Routine. Inspected 107 Inf'y Bde & 15 Bty 153 Bde	
		pm	Inspection completed 22 Sappers pack animals 107 Bde. M.V.S. Work.	
	16.3.17	am	Work at M.V.S. Inspected Tom'n Bengal Routine visited Rep & 30 pwi.	
		pm	Inspected Dn Sig'l Coy R.E.	
		pm	Mtd ADR saw surplus Inf'y Bde Annuals. Vety Conference M.V.S.	
			2 Army cases. Corps O re Rep programme. Div O again division.	
	17.3.17	am	Routine	
		pm	Routine	
	18.3.17	am	Routine visited Rep & Div B.	
		pm	Routine	
	19.3.17	am	Routine visited M.V.S.	
		pm	Routine visited Rep	
	20.3.17	am	Conference of ADVS's with DDVS. visited M.V.S. arranged evacuation by	
			was hayre	
		pm	Routine	
	21.3.17	am	Routine visited M.V.S. investigated & clearing arrangs & surplus animals	
		pm	visited A & OO IX Corps & Rep Routine	
	22.3.17	am	Inspected C 173 & 108th Inf'y Bde	
		pm	Routine	

WAR DIARY or INTELLIGENCE SUMMARY

Army Form C. 2118.

A.D.V.S.
MAR 1917
ULSTER DIVISION

Place	Date	Hour	Summary of Events and Information	Remarks and references to Appendices
Ballieul	23/3/17	am	Visited M.V.S. Saw animals for evacuation by barge. Visited Horse Dep. & 36 D.B.V.	
		pm	Routine. Vety Conference at 5:30 pm	
	24/3/17	am	Inspected D.B.P.C. Dy's 173 B.D. 108 M.G. Sect & Horses for Cavalry	
		pm	Visited 23 Vety Hospital. Routine	
	25/3/17	am	Routine	
		pm	Routine	
	26/3/17	am	ADVS Arriv-Div visited Dep Fm VS for information. Routine	
		pm	Routine	
	27/3/12	am	Inspected animals for evacuation at MVS visited Dep 36 D Corps D	
		pm	Visited Dep 9 36 D. Routine	
	28/3/17	am	Inspected No 1 Sec- DAC. 121 R.E. & 16 R.I.R Pioneers. Routine	
		pm		
	29/3/17	am	Routine	
		pm	Routine	
	30/3/17	am	Inspected Horses at MVS for evacuation. Inspected No 2 Sect DAC, visited Horse Dep.	
		pm	Routine. Conference of V.O's. DDVS 2 Army called. Visited Corps D.	
	31/3/17	am	Visited Horse Dep. 36 Div Q Trade carried inspection B Echelon DAC	
		pm	Routine	

A.S. Glover Major
ADVS 36th Division
31.3.17

WAR DIARY
or
INTELLIGENCE SUMMARY

Army Form C. 2118.

(Erase heading not required.)

Place	Date	Hour	Summary of Events and Information	Remarks and references to Appendices
BAILLEUL	1.4.17	Am	Routine visited Dep 36 Div Q	
		Pm	Routine	
	2.9.17	Am	Routine	
		Pm	Routine	
	3.4.17	Am	Routine Visited Gun pickets Bonnes at M.Y.S.	
		Pm	Routine	
	4.4.17	Am	Visited Dep TM Y.S. 9. 16. R.I.R. P.	
		Pm	Routine	
	5.4.17	Am	Visited Dep Corps 36 Div Q.	
		Pm	Routine	
	6.4.17	Am	Visited Dep Corps & inspected at M.Y.S.	
		Pm	Routine Conference of YO's	
St Jeans Cappel	7.4.17	Am	Moved HQrs Office to St Jeans Cappel	
		Pm	Routine	
	8.4.17	Am	Visited Dep 9 & 36 Div Routine	
		Pm	Routine	
	9.4.17	Am	Inspected 153 Bn R.F.A. with Capt Carmichael Routine	
		Pm	Routine	
	10.4.17	Am	Inspected 173 Bn R.F.A. with Capt McClintock Routine	
		Pm	Routine	
	11.4.17	Am	Routine visited Dep 9 & 36 Div. Contractor re new Office	
		Pm	Interviewed G.O.C. re feeding on trolled Vets. Heavy snow Routine	

WAR DIARY
or
INTELLIGENCE SUMMARY

Army Form C. 2118.

(Erase heading not required.)

Place	Date	Hour	Summary of Events and Information	Remarks and references to Appendices
St Leon April	12/4/17	a.m.	Inst DDR 2 Army on Cadres Parade. Routine	
		p.m.	Visited 36 D.A.C.R.A. & Dep. Routine	
	13/4/17	a.m.	Visited IX Corps & inspected a.m. V.S. Routine	
		p.m.	Routine Vety Conference visited Dep. Routine	
	14/4/17	a.m.	Routine visited Dep	
		p.m.	Routine inspected No 9 Coy A.S.C.	
	15/4/17	a.m.	Routine inspected No 2 Sect D.A.C.	
		p.m.	Routine	
	16/4/17	a.m.	Inspected No 1 Sect D.A.C. visited Dep & Q.	
		p.m.	Routine	
	17/4/17	a.m.	Snowing. Crow's 16th Div Cullen Routine	
		p.m.	Routine	
	18/4/17	a.m.	Snowing Routine	
		p.m.	Visited Q & Horse Dep.	
	19/4/17	a.m.	Inspected a.m. V.S. & 150 Coy R.E. & G.S. their arrangement arising to visit & inspect	
		p.m.	Routine	
	20/4/17	a.m.	Vety Conference visited Horse Dep.	
		p.m.	Routine	
	21/4/17	a.m.	Inspected Div Train at Ruump gm V.S.	
		p.m.	Routine	
	22/4/17	a.m.	Routine	
		p.m.	Routine	

Army Form C. 2118.

WAR DIARY
or
INTELLIGENCE SUMMARY

(Erase heading not required.)

Instructions regarding War Diaries and Intelligence Summaries are contained in F. S. Regs., Part II. and the Staff Manual respectively. Title Pages will be prepared in manuscript.

Place	Date	Hour	Summary of Events and Information	Remarks and references to Appendices
St Jean Cappel	April 23	am pm	} Routine	
	24/17	am pm	} Routine. Inspected a.m. V.S.	
	25/4/17	am pm	} Routine	
	26/4/17	am pm	} Routine	
	27/4/17	am pm	} Routine inspected 109 Supply Coln. 121 & 122 R.E.	
	28/4/17	am pm	Rode round Div main supplies & new sites for huts. Routine	
	29/4/17	am pm	} Routine	
	30/4/17	am pm	Routine. Inspected No 3 Sec DAC. Routine	

A J Horner Major
ADVS 36th Division 30/4/17

Army Form C. 2118.

WAR DIARY
or
INTELLIGENCE SUMMARY
(Erase heading not required.)

ADVS. 36th Division

Vol 20

Place	Date	Hour	Summary of Events and Information	Remarks and references to Appendices
St Jeans Cappel	1.5.17	Am / Pm	Routine	
	2.5.17	Am / Pm	Inspected D.173 108 & 109 in F. Corps / Routine	
	3.5.17	Am / Pm	Routine	
	4.5.17	Am / Pm	Routine / Interviewed 9 Div Eye Officer re Horse Eye Hosital Vety Congress	
	5.5.17	Am / Pm	Routine	
	6.5.17	Am / Pm	Routine	
	7.5.17	Am / Pm	Routine	
	8.5.17	Am / Pm	Routine return / Attending 9 gan Demonstration on use of Horse Eye Respirators "anti rain & Oppn"	
	9.5.17	Am / Pm	Hackney round Area Routine / Routine	
	10.5.17	Am / Pm	Inspected at M.V.S Routine / Routine	
	11.5.17	Am / Pm	Inspected 9 16 R.I.R.P. C. D.A 153 T+B On / No 1 S.U. D.A.C Vety Congress. Routine	

2449 Wt. W14957/M90 750,000 1/16 J.B.C. & A. Forms/C.2118/12.

Army Form C. 2118.

WAR DIARY
or
INTELLIGENCE SUMMARY

(Erase heading not required.)

Instructions regarding War Diaries and Intelligence Summaries are contained in F. S. Regs., Part II. and the Staff Manual respectively. Title Pages will be prepared in manuscript.

Place	Date	Hour	Summary of Events and Information	Remarks and references to Appendices
St Jans Cappel	12.5.17	Am	Inspected 107 Infy Bgde	
		Pm	Routine	
	13.5.17	Am	Routine inspected no 2 sect- D.A.C. 34th Div D.A.C.	
		Pm	Routine	
	14.5.17	Am	Inspected 173 Bgde R.F.A. 1 B. Bty 153 Bt. 7/10th Ind Amsterm	
		Pm	J. Routine	
Dranoutre	15.5.17	Am	Moved to West Camp Dranoutre Routine	
		Pm	Inspected Divisional Train Routine	
	16.5.17	Am	Met with Question of Mules Shoes. Inspected 109 T.A. Routine	
		Pm	Routine	
	17.5.17	Am	Routine	
		Pm		
	18.5.17	Am	Inspected 108th Infy Bde. M.M.P. New Signal Cor D.R.E. 118 An	
		Pm	Routine "Rly Conference Routine"	
	19.6.17	Am	Visited D/p not- D.D.VS 2 Army then Routine	
		Pm	Routine	
	20.5.17	Am	Routine	

WAR DIARY
or
INTELLIGENCE SUMMARY

(Erase heading not required.)

Army Form C. 2118.

Instructions regarding War Diaries and Intelligence Summaries are contained in F. S. Regs., Part II. and the Staff Manual respectively. Title Pages will be prepared in manuscript.

Place	Date	Hour	Summary of Events and Information	Remarks and references to Appendices
Wackencamp Dranoutre	21/5/17	Am	Routine. Visited Bde to meet R.S.M'S. Visited 1½ Brown.	
		Pm	Routine	
	22/5/17	Am	Routine	
		Pm		
	23/5/17	Am	Inspected at H.Y.S. Visited Bde located Army Artillery to see Clark eye.	
		Pm	To case Routine	
	24/5/17	Am	Visited Bde. not found. 1st & 2nd 32 Artillery	
		Pm	Visited R.S.M'S 2nd Army	
	25/5/17	Am	Inspected 76 & 78 A.F.A.B. Visited Bde.	
		Pm	Wely Conference Routine	
	26/5/17	Am	Visited Bde. R.S.M'S 11th Div called for Conference	
		Pm	Routine	
	27/5/17	Am	Routine Conference of a & F B's V.O's. Visited Inspected Camp for evacuation 32 Div Artillery	
		Pm	Camp studied spent night-attending to wounded horses.	

WAR DIARY
or
INTELLIGENCE SUMMARY

Army Form C. 2118.

Place	Date	Hour	Summary of Events and Information	Remarks and references to Appendices
Brigade	28/5	Am	Rode round Div Area seeing 70's & all Casualties	
		Am/Pm	Moved from Westn Camp to 109 Fld Ambulance	
Bullers	29/5	Am	Visited MYS next to 16 Bn MYS and DDMS 2 Army visited Horse Dpt	
		Pm	Routine	
	30/5	Am	Visited MYS examined 80 casualties for evacuation	
		Pm	Proceeded to colon to inspect remounts	
	31/5	Am	Left Cabour 11.0am arrived Boulogne 6 Pm visited DDR 2 Army on	
		Pm	return journey	

C.S. J'nor
Lt Colonel
ADMS 36 Div
Aug 31/17

Major OMC
ADMS NZ Div

Army Form C. 2118.

WAR DIARY
or
INTELLIGENCE SUMMARY
(Erase heading not required.)

Instructions regarding War Diaries and Intelligence Summaries are contained in F. S. Regs., Part II and the Staff Manual respectively. Title Pages will be prepared in manuscript.

Place	Date	Hour	Summary of Events and Information	Remarks and references to Appendices
Divisional Camp at Romarin	1/6/17	Am	Visited B. Routine	
		Pm	Yeoy Conference Routine	
	2/6/17	Am	Visited Horse Dep & D. IX Corps also Q 30 Div DDMS 2 Army cases infectious illness for Yeoy Clearing Station visits in Y.S. Romarin	
		Pm		
	3/6/17	Am	Routine Capt Smith AYC VO/C 32 Div Amm Col reported	
		Pm	Visited B. Routine	
	4/6/17	Am	Redistributed 103 Reinforcements to Divisions inspected at M.Y.S. visited Horse Dep	
		Pm	Routine visited Q 30 Div	
	5/6/17	Am	Ammunition Dump blown up by enemy. Visited by Capt Stevens AYC VO/C 76ATA	
		Pm	7/Maj Richardson AYC VO/C 32 Div Arthur Routine	
		Pm	Routine	
	6/6/17	Am	Visited Horse Dep 9m Y.S. visited Q 30 Div fired Advance Yeoy Aid Post.	
		Pm	Reconnoitred the tracks as CCS. had beans put up.	
	7/6/17	Am	Attack launched Spent day in front line attending to Pack	
		Pm	animals & any wounded.	
	8/6/17	Am	Visited Wytschaete Village spent day at front.	
		Pm	Yeoy Conference ADVS 32 Div called	

2449 Wt. W14957/Mgo 750,000 1/16 J.B.C. & A. Forms/C.2118/12.

Army Form C. 2118.

WAR DIARY
or
INTELLIGENCE SUMMARY

(Erase heading not required.)

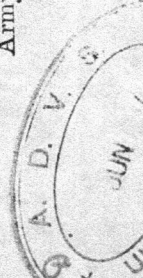

Place	Date	Hour	Summary of Events and Information	Remarks and references to Appendices
	9/6/17	Am	Visited A.Y. Post. M.Y.S.	
		Pm	Went to HQrs to interview Army's 2 Army Orders for Div to Comm. from action to unit.	
	10/6/17	Am	Visited IX Corps CCS. M.Y.S. Horse Dept. moved M.Y.S. to X6 C.9.	
	10/6/17	Pm	Kept Horse Dept. Hung Officer etc to old place on St Jean Capel.	
St Jean Capel	11/6/17	Am	Visited Q Horse Dep DMYS inspected 109 Infy Bde	
		Pm	Routine rang up 12 Q re Dep tried to get Divn to MDYS but failed Leaves Standards	
	12/6/17	Am	Rode round Div area inspected 107 & 108 Infy Bde execused Dep DMYS	
		Pm	Routine	
	13/6/17	Am	Visited 17 Corps Q re Horse Dep. Visited Horse Dep DMYS inspected no 3	
		Pm	Coy Div Train	
			Applied to OC 48 MYS duties of AMVS & routine re Dep Routine	
	14/6/17	Am	Proceeded on Special Leave to England.	
		Pm	Same out duties of AYSuT.	
	15/6/17	AM	Routine visited Horse dep	
		PM	Routine examine of NDs.	

Army Form C. 2118.

WAR DIARY
or
INTELLIGENCE SUMMARY

(Erase heading not required.)

Instructions regarding War Diaries and Intelligence Summaries are contained in F. S. Regs., Part II. and the Staff Manual respectively. Title Pages will be prepared in manuscript.

Place	Date	Hour	Summary of Events and Information	Remarks and references to Appendices
Jas Cnel	16/9/17	AM	Routine. Visit Horse dep.	
		PM	Routine. Visit Corps "Q". Iam vs & distribute 54 remounts.	
	17/9/17	AM	Routine. Visit Horse dep & hand over charge to ADVS 19th Div.	
		P.M.	Routine.	
	18/9/17	AM	Routine	
		PM	Routine	
	19/9/17	AM	Routine ADVS 11th Div Called.	
		PM	Routine	
	20/9/17	AM	Routine moves to M.35, D.2.5. Take over units from 11th & 16th Div.	
		PM	Routine	
	21/9/17	AM	Routine	
		PM	Routine	
	22/9/17	AM	Routine	
		PM	Routine Ampierre J.V.O	

WAR DIARY
or
INTELLIGENCE SUMMARY

Army Form C. 2118.

Place	Date	Hour	Summary of Events and Information	Remarks and references to Appendices
DRANOUTRE	23/6/17	AM	Routine	
		PM	Routine	
	24/6/17	AM	Routine	
		PM	Routine	
	25/6/17	AM	Routine	
		PM	DADVS returning from leave visits our Sister from Capt Chown ARC 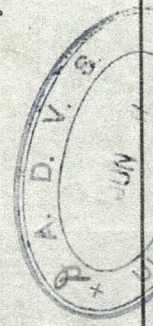	
	26/6/17	AM	Routine	
		PM	Routine	
	27/6/17	AM	Inspected at MVS invalid Horse Dep	
		PM	Routine	
	28/6/17	AM	Routine	
		PM	Routine	
	29/6/17	AM	Inspected No 1 2 & 3 Section DAC.	
		PM	Routine. Veky conference visiting ADVS's IX Corps & II Corps &	
	30/6/17	AM	H Qrs & Office DADVS moved to Neuve aux Pins lintre-ept RA R89 CavTrans in Neuve aux Capt McClintock & Connochie left with RA & R & huts.	
Neuve		PM	Routine	

A.L. Horne Major DADVS
36 Ulster Division

Army Form C. 2118.

WAR DIARY
or
INTELLIGENCE SUMMARY

(Erase heading not required.)

Instructions regarding War Diaries and Intelligence Summaries are contained in F. S. Regs., Part II. and the Staff Manual respectively. Title Pages will be prepared in manuscript.

Vol 22

Place	Date	Hour	Summary of Events and Information	Remarks and references to Appendices
Meaux	1.7.17	Am / Pm	Visited DDVS 2nd Army / Routine	
	2.7.17	Am / Pm	Ride round Divisional Area / Routine	
	3.7.17	Am / Pm	Inspected M.M.P. 108 M.G. Coy. 12 R.I.R. 11 R.I.R. 13 R.I.R. & R.I.R. 9 Guns Tn. 11 Buns Tn. 10 Buns Tn. 14 R.I.R. / Routine	
	4.7.17	Am / Pm	Inspected 107 Infy Bde / Routine	
	5.7.17	Am / Pm	Routine	
	6.7.17	Am / Pm	Sept. Memo 9 am marched via 11th Qualri Prison to Wizernes arriving 5 pm. Office functioning 5 pm. Routine. Motored round Div Area.	
Wizernes	7.7.17	Am / Pm	Routine / Routine	
	8.7.17	Am / Pm	Routine / Routine	
	9.7.17	Am / Pm	Motored round Div. Area inspected 108 T.A.M.V.S. saw into water question for 108 13th Tr. Transport.	
	10.7.17	Am / Pm	Routine	

2449 Wt. W14957/M90 750,000 1/16 J.B.C. & A. Forms/C.2118/12.

Army Form C. 2118.

WAR DIARY
or
INTELLIGENCE SUMMARY

(Erase heading not required.)

Instructions regarding War Diaries and Intelligence Summaries are contained in F. S. Regs, Part II. and the Staff Manual respectively. Title Pages will be prepared in manuscript.

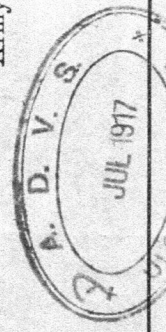

A. D. V. S.
7 JUL 1917
ULSTER DIVISION

Place	Date	Hour	Summary of Events and Information	Remarks and references to Appendices
Wzenrds	11/7/17	AM PM	} Routine	
	12/7/17		— Reverence Holiday	
	13/7/17	AM PM	} Routine. Capt. Whyte A.V.C. rep. Division becoming Surplus.	
	14/7/17	AM PM	} Went round all units	
	15/7/17	AM PM	} Routine.	
	16/7/17	AM PM	} Routine inspected at M.V.S.	
	17/7/17	AM PM	} Routine	
	18/7/17	AM PM	} Routine ADVS 19th Corps visited	
	19/7/17	AM PM	} Routine	
	20/7/17	AM PM	} Routine inspected Div HQ Bn. M.P. Squad. Am R.E. & M.V.S.	
	21/7/17	AM PM	Routine Visited all 3 Brigades.	

Army Form C. 2118.

WAR DIARY
or
INTELLIGENCE SUMMARY
(Erase heading not required.)

Instructions regarding War Diaries and Intelligence Summaries are contained in F. S. Regs., Part II. and the Staff Manual respectively. Title Pages will be prepared in manuscript.

A.D.V.S. ✶ JUL 1917 ✶ ULSTER DIVISION

Place	Date	Hour	Summary of Events and Information	Remarks and references to Appendices
Meteren	22/7/17	Am Pm	Reconnoitre Holiday & Zyywberne	
	23/7/17	Am Pm	Routine	
	24/7/17	Am Pm	Routine	
	25/7/17	Am Pm	Routine. Visit ADVS XIX Corps	
	26/7/17	Am Pm	Moved from Meteren to Winnezeele. Reel no 103. Inspected 122 Coy R.E & 9 odd annual guns 121 & 150 Coys. ADVS's Office. Inspected ADVS's XIX Corps map location	
	27/7/17	Am Pm	Inspected 121 R.E at Malo Routine Motored to new Div. area	
	28/7/17	Am Pm	Conference of ADVS's with ADVS 19 Corps. Routine inspected at MVS	
	29/7/17	Am Pm	Routine went to Gar Chance to East- Port Reprovision	
	30/7/17	Am Pm	Routine moved to MD16 Rue du Bouleque Poperinghe	
	31/7/17	Am Pm	Inspected 108 Mg. Coy. 108 Field Ambulance 9th R. Irish Fusiliers also visited MVS. Routine	

G. S. Downer Major ADVS 36th Ulster Div
31.7.17

WAR DIARY or INTELLIGENCE SUMMARY

Army Form C. 2118.

(Erase heading not required.)

VD 2923

A.D.V.S.
VD 280
3 / AUG 1917
ULSTER DIVISION

Place	Date	Hour	Summary of Events and Information	Remarks and references to Appendices
Poperinghe	1/8/17	AM	Routine visited B Branch Met Day	
		PM	Routine visited 19th Corps	
	2/8/17	AM	Wet Day Town being shelled Routine.	
		PM	Routine	
	3/8/17	AM	Routine	
		PM	ADVS ii Corps called visited 3rd Div Arty	
Mercey Camp	4/8/17	AM	Moved with Div HdQrs to Mercey Camp.	
		PM	Went to Proven to take over Remounts from 4 hours late.	
	5/8/17	AM	Routine MVS moved to 9.11 a.4.6 Camp Bounced saw 16 wounded animals at 150 R 2 Yules Those on advance very bad post at H.11.B.9.9. Routine	
		PM	Visited & inspected at MVS interviewed Capt Connoster. Thulin Routine	
	6/8/17	AM	Motor to Matou Inspected Div HdQrs next I can't move to MVS Routine	
		PM	ADVS 19th Corps visited for enquiry re many han interviewed Capt Miller C/O 15 RIR 9 RJ Inst inspected with ADVS 109 Infy Bd 9 m 4 Coy 108 Infy Bd. m 4 Coy. 15 RIR 9 RJ Inst Jun.	
	7/8/17	AM		
		PM	Routine.	
	8/8/17	AM	Inspected 107 Infy Bd Sec MrCoy 8th & 9 II CRIR. Completing all Infy Bd Sec. Visited MVS med to ADVS 55 Bn	
		PM	Visited Advance very Adv Post Routine	

Army Form C. 2118.

WAR DIARY
or
INTELLIGENCE SUMMARY
(Erase heading not required.)

Instructions regarding War Diaries and Intelligence Summaries are contained in F. S. Regs., Part II. and the Staff Manual respectively. Title Pages will be prepared in manuscript.

A. D. V. S.
9 AUG 1917
ULSTER DIVISION

Place	Date	Hour	Summary of Events and Information	Remarks and references to Appendices
Mussy Camp	9/8/17	Am	Inspected 50 horses at MVS for evacuation. Inspected No 2 Squad Traffic Control	@ MMP
		Pm	121 & 122 Coys R.E.. Reserve DAC.	
	10/8/17	Am	Routine	
		Pm	Inspected 108 & 110 Field Ambulances. 1st Royal Irish Fusiliers. MVS	
	11/8/17	Am	Routine. Conference of VO's.	
		Pm	Inspected at MVS 8/109 Field Ambulance. ADVS Corps inspected 150 R.E. with me	
	12/8/17	Am	Conference with ADVS 19th Corps.	
		Pm	Inspect Horses at MVS. Inspect Declovery horse supplies with Div Train must be destroyed	
	13/8/17	Am	36 Remounts at Proven	
		Pm	Routine	
	14/8/17	Am	Inspect with ADVS 19 Corps 100 horses for evacuation to MVD.	
		Pm	Routine	
	15/8/17	Am	Inspect 115 Remounts at Proven examined & destroyed their rail absence very bad	
		Pm	Post @ 36 VAC. Routine	
	16/8/17	Am	Visited & inspected at MVS Routine. Visited ADVS 19 Corps then to MVS to inspect 21 horses for evacuation	
		Pm	Visited & remained on road from St Jean to Willije from 7 till 11 Am inspected at AVA Posts	
			Met Remounts 15 at Proven Train C/E horses evac.	

WAR DIARY
or
INTELLIGENCE SUMMARY.
(Erase heading not required.)

Army Form C. 2118.

Place	Date	Hour	Summary of Events and Information	Remarks and references to Appendices
Mersey Camp	17/8/17	am	Met DADVS 41st Divn at 48th MVS. Inspd Horses & men. Took him to Advance VY.Cd post. Staff & our seen. Inspected Horses for evacuation at 48th VS. met ADVS 19 Corps this	
		pm	Examined surplus Div Horses 29 & returned same to advance trees Remount Section visited MVS Bananays for men.	
	18/17	am	Moved Office from Mersey Camp to Winnezeele	
Winnezeele		pm	Routine Visited MVS.	
	19/17	am	Rode round Div Area	
		pm	Routine visited MVS.	
	20/17	am	Routine	
		pm	Routine	
	21/17	am	Visited Area Commandant's at Watou Winnezeele & new location for MVS. Inspected 8th R.I.R. before disbanding. Saw M.M.P. horses	
		pm	Routine	
	22/17	am	Inspected at MVS & 107 Bde.	
		pm	Routine	
	23/17	am	Routine Office etc packed for move.	
		pm		
	24/17	am	En route motoring to Bavaster arrived 7 Pm.	
		pm		
Bavaster	25/17	am	Inspected 107, 108 Inf Bde. 150 R.E. & 109th A.	
		pm	Visited IV Corps preparing to ADVS selected spot for MVS & placed Sergt Barrett GVC i/c	
	26/17	am	Routine	
		pm		

Army Form C. 2118.

WAR DIARY
or
INTELLIGENCE SUMMARY.
(Erase heading not required.)

Instructions regarding War Diaries and Intelligence Summaries are contained in F. S. Regs., Part II. and the Staff Manual respectively. Title pages will be prepared in manuscript.

A.D.V.S. AUG 1917 ULSTER DIVISION

Place	Date	Hour	Summary of Events and Information	Remarks and references to Appendices
Baraolie	27/8/17	Am	Inspected animals of Div H.Q. Ors Signal Coy Tps.	
		Pm	Routine	
	28/8/17	Am	Visited Div Train saw air service inspected new site for M.V.S. not round	
		Pm	Div Que Routine	
	29/8/17	Am	Visited site of M.V.S. & Ticount of CADMVS4Corps met DDVS B. Army	
		Pm	Inspected 108 M.G. Coy & rode to Bonfarme to see Divisity detain	
	30/8/17	Am	Visited M.V.S. & Capt Chown O.C. M.V.S. in Hospital with parents. Came saw new site	
		Pm	Rode to 107 B & H.B. Ors viewing new area with DAOMC.	
Ytres	31/8/17	Am	Reconnoitred H.Q. Ors DDADVS moved to Ytres visited & inspected at M.V.S.	
			visited Corps	
		Pm	Routine	

A.S. Moncs Major.
DADVS 36th Ulster Division

31/8/17.

WAR DIARY
or
INTELLIGENCE SUMMARY.
(Erase heading not required.)

Army Form C. 2118.

Instructions regarding War Diaries and Intelligence Summaries are contained in F.S. Regs., Part II. and the Staff Manual respectively. Title pages will be prepared in manuscript.

A.D.V.S. 1 OCT 1917 ULSTER DIVISION

Place	Date	Hour	Summary of Events and Information	Remarks and references to Appendices
YPRES	1/9/17	am	Visited MVS & N Corps. Conference	
		pm	" HQrs. 109 Bde & 173 Bde.	
	2/9/17	am	Met ADVS Corps at MVS.	
		pm	Routine	
	3/9/17	am	Visited MVS. Inspected 153 Pr St RFA.	
		pm	Inspected 13 R.I.R. Mo 2 Coy Div Train	
	4/9/17	am	Inspected 36 Sig Coy. 15 R.I.R. & 108 Fd H⁹ Bn.	
		pm	Motor round area	
	5/9/17	am	Met DDVS 2 army @ ADVS 4 Corps. Inspect with them	
		pm	153, 9, 173 Bde RFA & 310 R.A.C.	
	6/9/17	am	Visit MVS.	
		pm	Routine	
	7/9/17	am	Inspect 121 R.Z. interview V.O's.	
		pm	Visit MVS. DVAC.	
	8/9/17	am	Conference at Corps. Visit MVS.	
		pm	Routine	
	9/9/17	am	Visit MVS.	
		pm	Routine	
	10/9/17	am	Visit MVS inspect horses for evacuation. Pay out men	
		pm		

(B.3841) OW.W.9735/M637 750,000 8/16 D.D.&L. Ltd. Forms/C.2118/13.

WAR DIARY
or
INTELLIGENCE SUMMARY.

Army Form C. 2118.

A.D.V.S. 1 OCT 1917 ULSTER DIVISION

Place	Date	Hour	Summary of Events and Information	Remarks and references to Appendices
YTRES	11/9/17	am	Visit Hennis & Beaumont	
		pm	Routine. Inspect Divi Signal Coy.	
	12/9/17	am	Visit M V S. & 107 F.S	
		pm	Visit M.V.S with R.E. to estimate amount of material wanted.	
	13/9/17	am	Morning at Y.S.	
		pm	Routine. meet A.D.V.S. II Corps at Horse Rly.	
	14/9/17	am		
		pm	} Routine.	
	15/9/17	am	Conference with A.D.V.S. visit M.Y.S.	
		pm	Routine	
	16/9/17	am	} Routine	
		pm		
	17/9/17	am	Routine	
		pm	Visit M.V.S. inspect.	
	18/9/17	am	All day absorbing B3 coming. Mood Horse.	
		pm		
	19/9/17	am	Visit M.V.S. inspect. 107 Sh.F.B. 4th inspected. Pay Out Office	
		pm	Routine	
	20/9/17	am	Visit M.V.S.	
		pm	Vety Conference Routine	

WAR DIARY
or
INTELLIGENCE SUMMARY.
(Erase heading not required.)

Army Form C. 2118.

Instructions regarding War Diaries and Intelligence Summaries are contained in F.S. Regs. Part II. and the Staff Manual respectively. Title pages will be prepared in manuscript.

A.D.V.S. ⁷ OCT 1917 ULSTER DIVISION

Place	Date	Hour	Summary of Events and Information	Remarks and references to Appendices
YTRES	21/9/17	am	Preliminary Committee IV Corps. Inspected 107 Bde with Corps Horsemaster	
		pm	Routine	
	22/9/17	am	Conference at Corps.	
		pm	Routine	
	23/9/17	am	Visited MVS	
		pm	Routine	
	24/9/17	am	Inspected 173 Bde RFA got rid of all tetanus	
		pm	Visited Corps MVS. Taken over duties of Corps BMVS temporarily	
	25/9/17	am	Inspected 153 Bde RFA	
		pm	Visited MVS 9 Corps	
	26/9/17	am	Inspected 108 Infy Bde. 16 R.I.R.P. ♀ 109 Bde	
		pm	Routine	
	27/9/17	am	Inspected DAC. 107 Infy Bde ♀121 R&.	
		pm	Visited 40 Division. Weekly conference Corps work wanted horse for Gen Nanier O/Wi	
	28/9/17	am	Inspected 108 FA 122 R& 108 M.G. Coy. Ths	
		pm	Routine	
	29/9/17	am	Conference at Corps. Visit MVS	
		pm	Routine	
	30/9/17	am		
		pm		

A.L. Jones Major
DADVS 36 Div 1/10/17

WAR DIARY
or
INTELLIGENCE SUMMARY.
(Erase heading not required.)

Army Form C. 2118.

Place	Date	Hour	Summary of Events and Information	Remarks and references to Appendices
YTRES	1/10/17	AM	Inspected Div Train B 110 & Amb.	Vol 25
		PM	Insp. M/S 9 Corps Routine	
	2/10/17	AM	Routine	
		PM	Routine	
	3/10/17	AM	Routine	
		PM	Insp M/S D Corps	
	4/10/17	AM	Routine	
		PM	Routine	
	5/10/17	AM	Proceed on 10 days leave and on duties as DADVS 36 Div to Capt Cameron avc	
		PM	Routine	
	6/10/17	AM	Routine Return to ADVS IV Corps.	
		PM	Routine	
	7/10/17	AM	Routine	
		PM	"	
	8/10/17	AM	Routine	
		PM	"	
	9/10/17	AM	Routine	
		PM	"	
	10/10/17	AM	Routine Insp gen v choloraha 77 Remounts at Hqrs SW Train	
		PM		

Army Form C. 2118.

WAR DIARY
or
INTELLIGENCE SUMMARY.
(Erase heading not required.)

Instructions regarding War Diaries and Intelligence Summaries are contained in F. S. Regs., Part II. and the Staff Manual respectively. Title pages will be prepared in manuscript.

Place	Date	Hour	Summary of Events and Information	Remarks and references to Appendices
YPRES	11/10/17	AM	Routine	
		PM	"	
	12/10/17	AM	Routine	
		PM	"	
	13/10/17	AM	Routine attend Conference ADVS Office	
		PM	"	
	14/10/17	AM	Routine	
		PM	"	
	15/10/17	AM	Routine	
		PM	"	
	16/10/17	AM	Routine	
		PM	"	
	17/10/17	AM	Routine	
		PM	"	
	18/10/17	AM	Major Horner resumes duties of DADVS Routine	
		PM		
	19/10/17	AM	Inspected 153 Bty RFA with Capt Connochie DMVS.	
		PM	Routine	

A.D.V.S. / YDs32 / 31 OCT 1917 / ULSTER DIV

WAR DIARY
or
INTELLIGENCE SUMMARY.
(Erase heading not required.)

Army Form C. 2118.

Place	Date	Hour	Summary of Events and Information	Remarks and references to Appendices
YPRES	20/X/17	am	Attend Conference of ADVS's at IV Corps. Visit M.V.S.	
		pm	Routine. Allied Pts. Clear meeting	
	21/X/17	am	Ricketti. Remounts at Paris.	
		pm	Routine	
	22/X/17	am	Visit & inspect at M.V.S. & 15 IV Corps to see ADVS. Inspect 2 Bhs.	
			173 B. RFA.	
		pm	Routine. Draw up circular re precautions for mange.	
	23/X/17	am	Routine	
		pm	Routine	
	24/X/17	am	Visit M.V.S. Meet American General there & show him round.	
		pm	Ricketti. Inspect 51 remounts at Paris.	
	25/X/17	am	Routine. Vety Conference.	
		pm	Routine	
	26/X/17	am	Inspected at M.V.S. Visited 173 B. 3rd RFA	
		pm	Routine	
	27/X/17	am	Attend Conference at IV Corps. Visited M.V.S. of 56 Div.	
		pm	Routine	
	29/X/17	am	Inspection of M.V.S. by DVS 3rd Army. DDVS 3rd Army. Major Wasley &	
			ADVS IV Corps	
		pm	Visit M.V.S. when AQMG inspected	

WAR DIARY
or
INTELLIGENCE SUMMARY.

(Erase heading not required.)

Army Form C. 2118.

Place	Date	Hour	Summary of Events and Information	Remarks and references to Appendices
YPRES	29/X/17	am / pm	Routine	
	30/X/17	am	Inspected 36 DAC. gd at MYS.	
		pm	Routine	
	31/X/17	am	Inspected 36 Div Signals, HQ 36 Div R.A. 7 R.I.R. 16 R.I.R (S) Div H.Qrs 9 mm P	
		pm	ADMS called 2:30 P.M. 150 R.B. 109 M.G.Coy. 14 R.I.R South Linn inspected 11 R. Innis Fus. 9 Inn. Fus. 10 th Inn Fus. (109 Lugby 13th)	

A.S. Tower
Major
DADVS 31.X.17

A.D.V.S.
YDS42
31 OCT 1917
ULSTER DIVISION

Army Form C. 2118.

WAR DIARY
or
INTELLIGENCE SUMMARY.
(Erase heading not required.)

Instructions regarding War Diaries and Intelligence Summaries are contained in F. S. Regs., Part II. and the Staff Manual respectively. Title pages will be prepared in manuscript.

Place	Date	Hour	Summary of Events and Information	Remarks and references to Appendices
YPRES	1.11.17	am	Inspected at MYS. motor round area	
		pm	Conference OsVO's. Routine	
	2.11.17	am	} Routine	
		pm		
	3.11.17	am	Allied Conference at IV Corps	
		pm	Routine ADVS IV Corps called	
	4.11.17	am	Routine	
		pm	ADVS IV Corps with 20th ADVS's calls Inspects MYS.	
	5.11.17	am	Routine	
		pm	Routine	
	6.11.17	am	Inspected 110 FA & MYS. motor round area.	
		pm	Routine interviews Corps Veterinarian	
	7.11.17	am	Rubislaw Inspd. 26 Pm 17am	
		pm	Routine	
	8.11.17	am	Go round Div area with AA&QMG.	
		pm	Routine & Vety Conference.	
	9.11.17	am	} Routine	
		pm		
	10.11.17	am	Conference at IV Corps	
		pm	Routine	
	11.11.17	am	Inspected 173 RFA & 103 Coy Div Train 9am 2 Redivn DAC.	
		pm	Rest horse area with AA&QMG.	
	12.11.17	am	Capt. O'Gurtin CVC reporting for duty vice Capt Cornwelius CVC proceeding to join 8W TCC BdC.	

WAR DIARY or INTELLIGENCE SUMMARY.

Army Form C. 2118.

Place	Date	Hour	Summary of Events and Information	Remarks and references to Appendices
YPRES	12/11/17	Pm	Recce round 153rd RFA visited MYS Review	
	13/11/17	Am	Inspected 11/13th R.I.R. 11/13th Supern animals 12th R.I.R. 10th MG Coy	
		Pm	9th R.I. Fus. 122 R.E. & 108 Fd Ambulance – Round area with AA90 MG &	
	14/11/17	Am	Office Routine. Inspected 7th R.I.R. rang up ADMS corps. Interviewed Capt Millar AVC	
			discharges from 68 7th R.I.R. with Jackie Gallant.	
		Pm	Visit MYS & Disp with ADMS IV Corps.	
	15/11/17	Am	Inspected 3rd DAC with Capt Quentin AVC	
		Pm	Vety Conference	
	16/11/17	Am	Routine	
		Pm		
	17/11/17	Am	Vety Conference at IV Corps	
		Pm	Routine Conference with OC 48th MVS.	
	18/11/17	Am	Select Site for Advance Vety Aid Post at Shell S.T.C. P&A reconnoitre tracks	
			& round for evacuation of sick. Visit MVS Conference with Capt Brown DO	
			51 Div MVS.	
		Pm	Routine. ADMS IV Corps called visit Raid Heed DMVS with them.	
	19/11/17	Am	Visit MVS Trust Wagon Lines inspect 2nd R.I.R. Thos'l Cay Div Train Ulster at	
		Pm	Yates –	
			Routine	
	20/11/17	Am	2 Ray Visit AD Post & Forward area see all VO's.	
		Pm	Visit AD Post & Forward Area Routine.	

WAR DIARY or INTELLIGENCE SUMMARY

Army Form C. 2118.

Place	Date	Hour	Summary of Events and Information	Remarks and references to Appendices
YTRES	21/11/17	am	Visit A.D. Post see all new Transport B.V.O's reconnoitre Havrincourt - Vélu etc. for site for new advance H.Q. A.D. Post - Routine	
		pm	Visit M.V.S. meet Col. McGowan Major Goodridge Enemy V.O's A.D.V.S IV Corps. Visit wounded horse of K.E.H. Routine visit suspect M.V.S.	
	22/11/17	am	Reconnoitre Gramecourt grazing ground see 3rd hussars at work inspect transport of Squadrons 122 R.F.A. B/113 13th R.F.A. Routine	
			Visit M.V.S. M.V.S. B/57 D.V.S. 3rd Army A.D.V.S IV Corps inspect Lines	
	23/11/17	am	Routine	
		pm	Routine	
	24/11/17	am	Allied Congress at IV Corps	
		pm	Routine Visit M.V.S.	
	25/11/17	am	Visit M.V.S. meet A.D.V.S IV Corps their visit - Herman & A.V. aid Post	
		pm	Routine	
	26/11/17	am	Visit M.V.S. inspect No 1 & 2 boys Rev. Team	
		pm	Visit advance H.Q. Post Routine. DADVS guards new cases.	
	27/11/17	am	Visit M.V.S. to withdraw Aid Post	
		pm	Routine	
	28/11/17	am	Visit M.V.S. A.D.V.S IV Corps cable orders to move	
		pm	Routine arrange for move visit D.A.C. see Capt Quentin	
	29/11/17	am	Move from YTRES to FOSSEUX motor lorries also report to A.D.V.S 17 Corps in person inspect 107 B.S. on march to his Sqdn. on arrival	
		pm		
	30/11/17	am	M.V.S. arrive at Foncourt inspect H.Q. Horses	
		pm	Routine preparing for move on Dec 1st	

A.L. Joiner Major DADVS
30/11/17 36 Ulster Division

WAR DIARY

INTELLIGENCE SUMMARY

(Erase heading not required.)

Army Form C. 2118.

D.A.D.V.S.
36TH
ULSTER DIVISION.
No VD741
Date 30.12.17

Instructions regarding War Diaries and Intelligence Summaries are contained in F. S. Regs., Part II. and the Staff Manual respectively. Title pages will be prepared in manuscript.

Place	Date	Hour	Summary of Events and Information	Remarks and references to Appendices
Advd H.Qrs. Lechelle	1/12/17	Am	On the March.	
Lechelle		Pm	Repaired to ADVS I Corps moved to Lechelle.	
Lechelle	2/12/17	Am	Visited MVS at Bradencourt called on ADVS I Corps. Inspected 3 supply Transport on March.	
		Pm	Visited MVS at Beer Factory Etricourt – V2 carried & anergy for 48 hrs to go their animals. bar for men etc	
	3/12/17	Am	Visited @ Office & M.V.S. Inspected 121 R.E. & 110 F.A.	
		Pm	Routine	
Scrd Hqrs and	4/12/17	Am	Orders to move to Somme & grand anergy accordingly	
		Pm	Met DADVS 29 Div may Pottery at Sorel & spand night in his camp repeat animals @ position of MVS to ADVS III Corps.	
	5/12/17	Am	Fry up quarters & Office. Inspect HQ Gr animals.	
		Pm	Inspected HMP. 150 R2 Mo 2 Coy. Dn Train & Repaired to ADVS III Corps.	
	6/12/17	Am	Office Routine	
		Pm	Routine	
	7/12/17	Am	Routine	
		Pm	Routine	
	8/12/17	Am	Visited ADVS III Corps	
		Pm	Inspected @ Distributed 19 Remounts	
	9/12/17	Am	Visited MVS & I Corps CCS	
		Pm	Routine	
	10/12/17	Am	Moved to Bapaume Branch Inspected 96 Remounts for RTA 30 Pon Tram & Proceeded	
		Pm	Routine	
	11/12/17	Am	Visited Supply Transport Wagon Lines DAC & inspected 1533 & 1131 RFA 2 x 250 VO's.	
		Pm	Routine	
	12/12/17	Am	Inspect 36 Div Signal Thrillingwood & Hussars	
		Pm	Routine	

Moore

Army Form C. 2118.

WAR DIARY
or
INTELLIGENCE SUMMARY.
(Erase heading not required.)

D.A.D.V.S.,
36TH
(ULSTER) DIVISION.

Place	Date	Hour	Summary of Events and Information	Remarks and references to Appendices
Sorel le Grand	13/12/17	Am	Go round area with A.A. & Q.M.G	
		Pm	Conference of V.O's	
	14/12/17	Am	Visit 36 DAC	
		Pm	Routine	
	15/12/17	Am	Inspect Divl Transport on the march with A.A & Q.M.G.	
		Pm	Visit & inspect 153rd Bde R.F.A	
	16/12/17	Am	Inspect Signals & move to LUCHEUX	
		Pm		
LUCHEUX	17/12/17	Am	Building Horses	
		Pm		
	18/12/17	Am	Visit villages in area with A.A & Q.M.G. report to A.D.V.S III Corps	
		Pm		
	19/12/17	Am	Inspect H.Q O7 Horses & 109 F.A. attd. to sick of each unit. M.V.S. at HUMBERCOURT	
		Pm		
	20/12/17	Am	See all H.Q & 7 Horses Fix up Office in new place	
		Pm	Routine	
	21/12/17	Am	Routine in quarters with cold & flu	
		Pm		
	22/12/17	Am	Routine	
		Pm		
	23/12/17	Am	Routine	
		Pm		
	24/12/17	Am	Routine DADVS attended to no 3 CANADIAN STATIONARY HOSPITAL DOULLENS	
		Pm		
	25/12/17	Am	duties taken on by Capt. CHOWN.	
		Pm		

Renlin

Army Form C. 2118.

D.A.D.V.S.,
36TH
(ULSTER DIVISION).

WAR DIARY
or
INTELLIGENCE SUMMARY.
(Erase heading not required.)

Instructions regarding War Diaries and Intelligence Summaries are contained in F. S. Regs., Part II. and the Staff Manual respectively. Title pages will be prepared in manuscript.

Place	Date	Hour	Summary of Events and Information	Remarks and references to Appendices
HENEUX 26/9/17	26/9/17	am	Routine	
		pm	"	
	27/9/17	am	Edition of 10th & CORBIE arrive 7pm	
		pm	Routine. AF A.2003 6 ADVS XVIII CORPS	
	28/9/17	am	M.V.S. moves into CORBIE.	
		pm	Routine. See DDVS 5th Army.	
	29/9/17	am	Routine	
		pm	"	
	30/9/17	am	Routine. Visit Thiepval. 121 RE 2(4) RSC BN HARE.	
		pm	"	
	1/9/17	am	Routine. Visit Thiepval 107 INF BDE V/10 FIELD Ambulance	
		pm	"	

JMoore

Army Form C. 2118.

D.A.D.V.S. 36TH (ULSTER) DIVISION.
No. 17.820
Date 31.1.18

WAR DIARY or INTELLIGENCE SUMMARY.
(Erase heading not required.)

Place	Date	Hour	Summary of Events and Information	Remarks and references to Appendices
CORBIE	1/1/18	Am	Routine	
		Pm	"	
	2/1/18	Am	Routine. Visit ADVS XVIII CORPS.	
		Pm	"	
	3/1/18	Am	Routine. ADVS XVIII CORPS inspects MVS.	
		Pm	"	
Corbie	4/1/18	Am	Reported for duty after 10 days in Hospital at Doullens. Met ADVS 18 Corps & visited 36 Div Artly with him. Saw vet days & civilian horses will meaup.	
			visited sam. Inspected No 2 Coy A.S.C.	
		Pm	Visited & inspected at 48 M.V.S.	
	5/1/18	Am	Inspected with ADVS 18 Corps 36 DAC & Div Artly	
		Pm	Routine	
	6/1/18	Am	Visited M.V.S. Inspected 10 R.I.R. & 110 FA	
		Pm	Routine	
HARBONNIERES	7/1/18	Am	Move from Corbie to HARBONNIERES. inspected en route No 2 Coy A.S.C. 110 FA 109 Infty Bde & 16 R.I.R. Picoures.	
	8/1/18	Am	Visited with AA & QMG, 36 Div Forward Area. Inspected Stables & French Cavalry	
		Pm	& TRAIN animals for contagious disease & arrange for destruction of stabling etc	

Army Form C. 2118.

D.A.D.V.S.
36TH
(ULSTER) DIVISION.
No ....
Date ....

WAR DIARY
or
INTELLIGENCE SUMMARY.
(Erase heading not required.)

Instructions regarding War Diaries and Intelligence Summaries are contained in F.S. Regs., Part II. and the Staff Manual respectively. Title pages will be prepared in manuscript.

Place	Date	Hour	Summary of Events and Information	Remarks and references to Appendices
HARBONN IERES	9/1/18	am	Inspd. Signal Coy 36 Div. Div H.Q. & No 304 A.S.C.	
		pm	Amiens for Tnpt Cup.	
	10/1/18	am	Offrs Inspd. 108 Infy Bn & 108 TA Routine	
		pm	Routine	
	11/1/18	am	Routine	
		pm		
	12/1/18	am	Moved from Hentenniers to Huzé	
		pm	Inspected MOI Coy Div Train	
	13/1/18	am	Inspd. in V.S. Routine	
		pm	Routine	
"	14/1/18	am	Moved from Huzé to OLLEZY	
		pm	Routine	
OLLEZY	15/1/18	am	Rode round Area inspecting stables at Cugny, Douilly, Flaviers & Rouez	
		pm	Routine	
	16/1/18	am	Inspd. at M V.S. Unit ADVS 18 Corps at HAM.	
		pm	Routine	
	17/1/18	am	Visit St Simon Cullery & Grand Serencourt inspecting stables with ADDHS.	
		pm	Vety Conference Offrs Routine	
	18/1/18	am	Visit ADVS 18 Corps	
		pm	ADVS Corps calls Inspd. Amn unit transport 147 A Bg & BAC 145 HB RGA	
	19/1/18	am	Inspd. D143 RFA & 122 RE also sick at M.V.S.	
		pm	Routine	

Army Form C. 2118.

WAR DIARY
or
INTELLIGENCE SUMMARY.
(Erase heading not required.)

Instructions regarding War Diaries and Intelligence Summaries are contained in F. S. Regs., Part II. and the Staff Manual respectively. Title pages will be prepared in manuscript.

D.A.D.V.S.,
36TH
(ULSTER) DIVISION.
No ....
Date ....

Place	Date	Hour	Summary of Events and Information	Remarks and references to Appendices
OLLEZY	20/1/18	am	Office Routine	
		pm	Routine	
	21/1/18	am } pm }	Routine	
	22	am	Inspect 173 Bde RFA	
		pm	" 153 Bde RFA	
	23	am	Inspect 106 FA 121 R2 unit A.D.V.S 18 Corps	
		pm	" 109 3A 107 & 109 Infy Bde Office. 16 R I "P" 150 R2 266 M.G. Coy	
	24	am	Inspect 36 DAC. D.M.V.S.	
		pm	Vety Conference.	
	25	am	Inspect 107 106 & 109 M.G. Coys 107 H.Q. 122 R2 No 2 Coy A.S.C	
		pm	11/13 Rifles & 2 Rifles Officers	
	26	am	Inspect 12 Rifles Stolen animals of 107 & 108 Bde not seen at present	
		pm	Inspection	
	27	am } pm }	Routine	
	28	am	Routine	
		pm	Routine	
	29	am	Inspect 147A Bde & BAC.	
		pm		
	30	am	Take over duties of A.D.V.S 18 Corps whilst he is on leave.	
		pm	Routine	
	31	am	Inspect M.V.S. 36 Div Squads, M.M.P. No 2 Traffic Control Squad, HQ 2 R5 VRA	
		pm	Corps Duties. Routine	

A.L. Dorner Major DADVS 36 Division
Field 31·1·18.

WAR DIARY
or
INTELLIGENCE SUMMARY.
(Erase heading not required.)

Army Form C. 2118.

D.A.D.V.S.,
36TH
(ULSTER) DIVISION.
No. V.2/630
Date 28.2.18

Instructions regarding War Diaries and Intelligence Summaries are contained in F.S. Regs., Part II. and the Staff Manual respectively. Title pages will be prepared in manuscript.

Place	Date	Hour	Summary of Events and Information	Remarks and references to Appendices
OLLEZY	1/2/18	am	Attend Conference of A.D.V.S's with D.D.V.S. 2nd Army, at Office of A.D.V.S. 18th Corps.	
		pm	Routine.	
	2/2/18	am	Visited Antwerp. Inspected many cases with Capt. Muller. Inspected at M.V.S.	
		pm	Corps work for A.D.V.S. 18th Corps.	
	3/2/18	am	Inspected water arrangements for animals in this forest. Necessary suggestions to A.A. & Q.M.G.	
		pm		
	4/2/18	am	Routine.	
		pm	Inspected 179 B.T. A.T.A. for A.D.V.S. Corps. Visited here to find sites for CCS.	
	5/2/18	am	Routine at Antwerp.	
		pm	Attended Officers' Sergeant. Visited mule kennels to find CCS sites.	
	6/2/18	am	Inspected 10th Innis. Fus. T.M.V.S.	
		pm	" 96 Remounts for this City. Visit 18th Corps work.	
	7/2/18	am	See work at this H.Q. An. Office.	
		pm	Veterinary Conference. Visit Corps. Routine.	
	8/2/18	am	Visit Corps Conference of A.T.A. & Y.O's.	
		pm	Reports. Training. Routine.	
	9/2/18	am	Inspected animals at M.V.S. Routine.	
		pm	Phil. Corps. Reports. Training. Routine.	

D.A.D.V.S.
36TH
(ULSTER) DIVISION.

Army Form C. 2118.

WAR DIARY
or
INTELLIGENCE SUMMARY.
(Erase heading not required.)

Instructions regarding War Diaries and Intelligence Summaries are contained in F.S. Regs. Part II. and the Staff Manual respectively. Title pages will be prepared in manuscript.

Place	Date	Hour	Summary of Events and Information	Remarks and references to Appendices
OLEZZY	10/2/18	Am	Vest Corps Stand own duties to ADVS 18th Corps	
		Pm	Routine	
	11/2/18	Am	Vest Tingny & Attempt Inspect Watering Ponds	
		Pm	Visit Cugny There	
	12/2/18	Am	Visit St Simon. Attempt Stop uncut with ACO & nq Inspect	
		Pm	Transport at Tingny. Visit- 145 H.By Section 19 Reserve Park TMYS. ADVS Corps Calls Inspect HQ 10th Rifles 15 Rifles 181 Rifles 8 q Fusiliers	
	13/2/18	Am	Inspect 109 D108 15th HQ Vest HCm with ACO & nq Gy	
		Pm	Routine	
	14/2/18	Am	Vest. Attempt D.of Seaucourt. Vet. Div Riding School	
		Pm	Veterinary Conference. Routine	
	15/2/18	Am	Reports & Returns. Routine	
		Pm	Routine. Leave 4 p.m. for 4 days Paris leave landing own duties of a/ADVS to Capt. McClintock A.V.C.	
	16/2/20	Am	Routine. Daily Return to Riding Class. Returned from leave 11.30 20.2.18.	
		Pm		
	21 Am		Vest St Simon & Attempt 2nd Riding Class Inspect 181 Inniss Fusiliers	
		Pm	Veterinary Conference Reports & Returns routine.	
	22	Am	Inspect Det. 119 ATA with No1 Cry Q.A.S.C. Vest ADVS Corps.	
		Pm	Routine.	

WAR DIARY or INTELLIGENCE SUMMARY

Army Form C. 2118.

D.A.D.V.S.
36TH
(ULSTER) DIVISION

Place	Date	Hour	Summary of Events and Information	Remarks and references to Appendices
OLLEZY	23/2/18	Am	Inspect Riding Class. Inspect 1st & 15 R.I.R. 9th Inns Fusiliers	
		Pm	Conference at A.D.V.S's Office	
	24/2/18	Am	See new HQ horses. Routine	
		Pm	Routine. Prepare Honours & Awards List	
	25/2/18	Am	Inspect 173 Bde R.F.A. Great improvement since last inspection	
		Pm	Routine	
	26/2/18	Am	Inspect & distribute 42 Remounts received for Division	
		Pm	Test Riding School Course. Very smart. Routine	
	27/2/18	Am	Inspect 30 DAC with V.O. & M.V.S.	
		Pm	Routine	
	28/2/18	Am	Go round area with A.D.V.S. H.Q. Very clean	
		Pm	Routine. Vety Conference	

C.S. Jones Major
D.A.D.V.S. 36(Ulster) Division
28.2.18.

WAR DIARY
or
INTELLIGENCE SUMMARY.

(Erase heading not required.)

Army Form C. 2118.

D.A.D.V.S.,
36TH
(ULSTER DIVISION).
No. VD7709
Date 27. 6. 18

Place	Date	Hour	Summary of Events and Information	Remarks and references to Appendices
Olleezy	1·3·18	am	Inspect 109 B Bty; 153 B Jr.	
		Pm	Routine	
	2·3·18	am	Routine	
		Pm	Visit ADVS 18th Corps.	
	3·3·18	am	Routine	
		Pm	Rode round Division with A.D.M.S.	
	4·3·18	am	Inspect 107. 108 & 109 Inghy Bdes. 108 109 & 110 Jy Ambulances. Inspect 48 M.V.S.	
		Pm	121 & 122 Bde. 16 R.I.R"P". 36 M.G. Balln. met ADVS Corps.	
	5·3·18	am	Inspect 9th R.I.F. 1st R.I.3. 108 H.Q. 150 R.E.	
		Pm	Routine	
	6·3·18	am	Routine	
		Pm	Visit Corps to meet DVS at ADVS's Office	
	7·3·18	am	Inspect C DNS Btys R.F.A. 153 B. & D Bty 232 CFA.Ys.	
		Pm	Tele. Conference. Visit ADVS 18 Corps.	
	8·3·18	am	Inspect No 3 Coy Div Train HQ. 36 Syndn. M.M.P. & Traffic Control	
		Pm	Inspect 1.2 & 4 Coys Div Train.	

WAR DIARY
or
INTELLIGENCE SUMMARY.

Army Form C. 2118.

D.A.D.V.S.,
36TH
(ULSTER) DIVISION.

(Erase heading not required.)

Instructions regarding War Diaries and Intelligence Summaries are contained in F. S. Regs., Part II. and the Staff Manual respectively. Title pages will be prepared in manuscript.

Place	Date	Hour	Summary of Events and Information	Remarks and references to Appendices
OLLEZY	9.3.18	am pm	Routine	
	10.3.18	am pm	Routine. Called on ADVS 18 Corps.	
	11.3.18	am pm	Routine	
	12.3.18	am	Visit all V.Os: inspected MVS.	
		pm	Moved Office to new building vacated by D.A.Q.	
	13.3.18	am	Inspect. A.V. & H.Q. 153 Rgt.	
		pm	Examine Railway Horses.	
	14.3.18	am	Visit 21, 22 & 23 Rutenlung Ball:' reld. & R.Sny horses.	
		pm	Conferences VOs	
	15.3.18	am pm	Routine	
	16.3.18	am pm	Routine	

A.D.V.S.,
36TH
(ULSTER) DIVISION.

Army Form C. 2118.

WAR DIARY
or
INTELLIGENCE SUMMARY.
(Erase heading not required.)

Place	Date	Hour	Summary of Events and Information	Remarks and references to Appendices
Villers	17.3.18	A.M. P.M.	J Rawlins	
	18.3.18	A.M.	Left for me on 14 days leave. Handed over to O.C. 48 M.V.S.	
		P.M.	Saw n chiefs J.D.D.V.S. & Major Horne re leave	
	18/3/18	A.M.		
		P.M.	Routine	
	19/3/18	A.M.		
		P.M.	Routine	
	20/3/18	A.M.		
		P.M.	Routine	
	21/3/18	A.M.	German offensive commenced 4.40 P.M. arrange fields from M.V.S.	
		P.M.	arrange evacuation to corps C.C.S. of all wounded cobs	
	22/3/18	A.M.	Move to FRICHES. Mobile sectin at ESMERY HALLON	
		P.M.	Section gone march to LIERS'RMONT	
	23/3/18	A.M.	Move to BEAULIEU. Meet all V.Os. Skipped all sick transport in	
		P.M.	line of march. Mobile Section S.D.C.	

WAR DIARY
or
INTELLIGENCE SUMMARY.
(Erase heading not required.)

Army Form C. 2118.

D.A.D.V.S.,
36TH
(ULSTER) DIVISION.

Instructions regarding War Diaries and Intelligence Summaries are contained in F.S. Regs., Part II. and the Staff Manual respectively. Title pages will be prepared in manuscript.

Place	Date	Hour	Summary of Events and Information	Remarks and references to Appendices
	24/3/18	am	Section moved to GUISCOURT. Inspd 153 V 173 Bdr R.F.A.	
		pm	Rode to ROYE to see ADVS XVIII CORPS.	
	25/3/18	am	Inspect arrival of 432, 433 Btty with Lieut NIELSON	
		pm	Move to GUERBEAUCOURT.	
	26/3/18	am	Line tried with 5 in ARTY. TVO's Capt McCLINTOCK & GUERTIN	
		pm	BTV HQrs. move to SOURDON.	
	27/3/18	am	Try & find DRTY & Col. unsuccessful. See Capt. MILLAR & evacuation	
		pm	Inspect all corps XIV TRAIN.	
	28/3/18	am	Inspect detachment 18th Reserve Park. Set up a renewal fm SDC.	
		pm	Inspect FIELD AMBULANCES	
	29/3/18	am	Bn! HQrs moves WAILLY.	
		pm	Section moves to TAISNIL.	
	30/3/18	am	Move to GAROCHES area.	
		pm		
	31/3/18	am	Arrange for evacuation of sick animals.	
		pm		

Army Form C. 2118.

WAR DIARY
or
INTELLIGENCE SUMMARY.
(Erase heading not required.)

D.A.D.V.S.
36TH
(ULSTER) DIVISION.

No. 101226/10

Place	Date	Hour	Summary of Events and Information	Remarks and references to Appendices
GOMMECOURT	1/4/18	AM	Routine	
		PM	Routine	
	2/4/18	AM	Routine. Visit Ant. Hops. in Msyn Boreyson Area	
		PM	Routine	
	3/4/18	AM	Routine	
		PM	Three sick Return to FEUQUIERES	
	4/4/18	AM	Leave FEUQUIERES 10AM	
		PM	—	
	5/4/18	AM	Arrive PROV. 2.15 PM. arrange for orders to move to ETRICOURT GH.6 Pa.	
		PM	Div HQ 10.9 Pms Camp Swiss Roads.	
	6/4/18	AM	Visit expand to ADVS II CORPS.	
		PM	Arrange to move orders to Hastings J 2nd NYS. 1st Aust.	
	7/4/18	AM	Major Hope Return from leave, orders Adv. Y/STAPRS. Report to ADVS II Corps	
		PM	Inspect HQ Th M P Horses	
	8/4/18	AM	Moved from Div Elms Camp to Dullallow Camp. Canal Bank YPRES.	
		PM	Visit NBMVS at Pb 13 to Div Sig Coy DHQ B & 3. Inspect 30 Div Sig Coy DHQ	Sheet 28

WAR DIARY
or
INTELLIGENCE SUMMARY.
(Erase heading not required.)

Army Form C. 2118.

D.A.D.V.S.
36TH
(ULSTER DIVISION).
No _____
Date _____

Instructions regarding War Diaries and Intelligence Summaries are contained in F. S. Regs., Part II. and the Staff Manual respectively. Title pages will be prepared in manuscript.

Place	Date	Hour	Summary of Events and Information	Remarks and references to Appendices
Canal Bank YPRES.	9.4.18	am	Inspected M.V.S. go round area with AQQMG.	
		pm	Interviews Y.O's. Routine	
"	10/4/18	am	} Routine	
		pm		
	11/4/18	am	} Routine	
		pm		
	12/4/18	am	Interviews Capt Miller A.V.C. Inspected HQ horses. D Sqdn evacuati on cars from cable head.	
		pm	Visit new Camp & see Horse Standings. Make arrangements etc. Visit ADVS II Corps.	
Dragon Camp	13/4/18	am	Move from Canal Bank. Any Duti to Dragon Camp. Proven Road as part of B Echelon Div H.Q.	
		pm	Office settle in. Inspect H.Q. Horses.	
	14/4/18	am	Conference of V.O's including V.O's of 1st Div Arty	
		pm	Routine	
	15/4/18	am	Spend morning at MVS inspecting sick cases for evacuation.	
		pm	Reconnaitre for MVS site di cd on ? 13 D Central Sheet 27.	
	16/4/18	am	Routine	

Army Form C. 2118.

D.A.D.V.S.
36TH (ULSTER) DIVISION.
No ....

WAR DIARY
or
INTELLIGENCE SUMMARY.
(Erase heading not required.)

Instructions regarding War Diaries and Intelligence Summaries are contained in F. S. Regs., Part II. and the Staff Manual respectively. Title pages will be prepared in manuscript.

Place	Date	Hour	Summary of Events and Information	Remarks and references to Appendices
DRAGON CAMP	16.4.18	PM	Prospect round Prom 10.30 PM memos from O.C 48M/S saying an place was being shelled	
			Saw B.G. Div Munich = Orders arranged for it to move at once to 3/13 D Central Sheeting	
	17.4.18	AM	Visit M/S at 3/13 D Central Routine	
		PM	Reconnanti back area for shown UL to GCB&G	
	18.4.18	AM	Routine	
		PM	Conferences of YOs	
	19.4.18	AM	Visit LBM/S inspect Ho 2 Coy Bir Train & 2ND R.I.R	
		PM	Routine - Reports & returns	
	20.4.18	AM	Routine inspect M.P Bn'H.Q. & L Squads	
		PM	Visit ADVS = Corps Routine	
	21.4.18	AM	Routine	
		PM	Routine	
	22.4.18	AM	Go round Res Area with A.C.T Q.M.G inspect gas supplies changes	
		PM	Routine	
	23.4.18	AM	Inspects 9 G.I.R 12 R.I.R 36 In G Bath 9 G.I.R In G Fuseliers	
		PM	Routine	

Army Form C. 2118.

D.A.D.V.S.
36TH
(ULSTER) DIVISION.
No

WAR DIARY
or
INTELLIGENCE SUMMARY.
(Erase heading not required.)

Instructions regarding War Diaries and Intelligence
Summaries are contained in F. S. Regs., Part II.
and the Staff Manual respectively. Title pages
will be prepared in manuscript.

Place	Date	Hour	Summary of Events and Information	Remarks and references to Appendices
Dragoncamp	24/4/18	Am	Inspect 109 I.B. 16 R.I.R, P. 150, 122 & 121 R & 15 R I R 107 H Qn	
		P.M.	1st F. Bank Inspect 18 R I R 2 R.I.R 9th R.I.R Dundonion Roulin	
	25.4.18	Am	Roulin	
		P.M	Vety Conference 2.30 P.M.	
	26.4.18	Am	Inspect No 1 & No 2 Div Amn Column also Hq Qrs	
		P.M	Report's Various Roulin	
X Camp	27.4.18	Am	Move Office & Bagg to X Camp at A16 C 2.3. Sheet 28. No Billeting in Roulinvilli	
		P.M.	5 & Remounts to Divizion Inspect MVS Inspect No 1.2.3 & 4 Coy 36 Vann	
	28/4/18	Am	Routine	
		P.M	Roulin	
	29/4/18	Am	Inspect Div HQ horses Roulin	
La LOVIE		P.M	Move to La Lovie Chateau Proven Roulin set up Office etc	
	30/4/18	Am	Inspect HQ horses & M.V.S	
		P.M	Visit ADVS II Corps.	

A.S. Turner Major. A.V.C.
D.A.D.V.S. 36 Ulster Division
30.4.18

Army Form C. 2118.

D.A.D.V.S.
36TH
(ULSTER DIVISION)

No V9/1405
Date 1.6.18

Original

Vol 32

WAR DIARY
or
INTELLIGENCE SUMMARY.

(Erase heading not required.)

Instructions regarding War Diaries and Intelligence Summaries are contained in F.S. Regs., Part II. and the Staff Manual respectively. Title pages will be prepared in manuscript.

23

Place	Date	Hour	Summary of Events and Information	Remarks and references to Appendices
LA LOVIE CHATEAU	May 1st	A.M.	Routine	
		P.M.	Visit ADVS II Corps	
	2nd	A.M.	Visit 181 Irish Fuslrs to investigate death & sickness Vet A.A. D.m.g. Select Water in Corps Squivir	
		P.M.	Veterinary Conference	
	3rd	A.M.	Inspect 36 Div Signals Mtd H.Q.	
		P.M.	Routine	
	4th	A.M.	Routine	
		P.M.	Inspect 199 Remounts sent to Div Artry. Visit Q.	
	5th	A.M.	} Routine	
		P.M.		
	6th	A.M.	Routine	
		P.M.		
	7th	A.M. P.M.	Routine	
	8th	A.M.	Visit Tilques select. chargrs for new Q.O.C.	
		P.M.	Routine	
	9th	A.M.	Move to Coullove Chatian Inspect Div H & Horses. Visit Q.	
Coullove Chatian		P.M.	Vety Conference O.M.C	

Army Form C. 2118.

WAR DIARY
or
INTELLIGENCE SUMMARY.
(Erase heading not required.)

Instructions regarding War Diaries and Intelligence Summaries are contained in F. S. Regs., Part II. and the Staff Manual respectively. Title pages will be prepared in manuscript.

D.A.D.V.S.,
30TH
(30TH) DIVISION

Place	Date	Hour	Summary of Events and Information	Remarks and references to Appendices
Couturt Château	10/5/18	Am	Inspect. B.153, C.173, D.173, D.153, C.153, & B.173 Btys R 7A.	
		PM	Office Routine	
	11/5/18	Am	Conference with ADVS II Corps	
		PM	Inspected with ADVS II Corps 48 MYS. 15 R.I.R. & 30 M.G. Bathn.	
	12/5/18	Am	Routine	
		PM		
	13	Am	Inspect. Rear Wagon Lines of A 173 & A 153 & forward Lines of	
		PM	B 153, A 173, D 173, D 153, C 153, A 153. Office Routine etc.	
	14	Am	Inspected in detail 48 MYS. Men, horses, arms, equipment, transport etc.	
		PM	Routine.	
	15	Am	Inspect 122 A.B. 16 R.I.R. "P" SAA Sect. DAC. 108 & 110 Field Ambulances	
		PM	Routine	
	17	Am	Routine Inspect. Div HQ	
		PM	Routine	
	16	AM PM	Routine	
	17	AM PM	Routine	

Army Form C. 2118.

D.A.D.V.S.
36TH
(ULSTER) DIVISION.

WAR DIARY
or
INTELLIGENCE SUMMARY.
(Erase heading not required.)

Instructions regarding War Diaries and Intelligence Summaries are contained in F. S. Regs., Part II. and the Staff Manual respectively. Title pages will be prepared in manuscript.

Place	Date	Hour	Summary of Events and Information	Remarks and references to Appendices
COOTHOVE	20/5/18	am	Inspect MVS.	
		Pm	Visit DADVS 4th Div.	
	21/5/18	am	See all VO's. Inspect Div HQ.	
		Pm	Routine	
	22/5/18	am	Go to ADVS II Corps. Then Visit DDVS II Army. Inspect with MVS.	
		Pm	Routine	
	23/5/18	am	Inspected at MVS. Visit No 2 & 22 B.V.S.	
		Pm	Conference of VO's.	
	24/5/18	am	Visit & inspect DHQ Annexe	
		Pm	Routine	
	25/5/18	am	Visit ADVS II Corps.	
		Pm	Leave.	
	26/5/18	am	Leave.	
		Pm	Inspect 32 Remount cases for carting by NBR.	
	27/5/18	am	Inspect 107, 108 & 109 Infy Bdes. MG Bn. 121, 122, 150 R.E. No 3 Sd DAC.	
		Pm	also inspect & distribute 32 Remounts.	

Army Form C. 2118.

WAR DIARY
or
INTELLIGENCE SUMMARY.

(Erase heading not required.)

Instructions regarding War Diaries and Intelligence Summaries are contained in F. S. Regs., Part II. and the Staff Manual respectively. Title pages will be prepared in manuscript.

D.A.D.V.S., 36TH (ULSTER DIVISION). No.............

Place	Date	Hour	Summary of Events and Information	Remarks and references to Appendices
COUTHOVE	28/5/18	Am	Inspd. no 1 & 2 Sub. D.A.C. & 16 R.I.R. "P"	
		Pm	Routine.	
	29/5/18	Am	Inspd. 108, 109 & 110 Field Ambulances Routine.	
		Pm	Inspd. 50 Remounts sent for Du Culy	
	30/5/18	Am	Inspd. at 48 M.V.S.	
		Pm	Veterinary Conference Visit ADVS II Corps inspd. with him 150 R & 1st Gren. Grds	
	31/5/18	Am	Inspd. at 48 M.V.S.	
		Pm	Routine Reports & returns	

A.J. Turner Major (actg)
D.A.D.V.S. 36th (Ulster) Division
31.5.18

WAR DIARY
or
INTELLIGENCE SUMMARY.

Army Form C. 2118.

(Erase heading not required.)

D.A.D.V.S.—
36TH
(ULSTER) DIVISION.
No. WD 1537
Date 1 / 7 / 18

VD 33

26

Place	Date	Hour	Summary of Events and Information	Remarks and references to Appendices
OUTHOVE CHATEAU.	June 1st	am.	Visit A.D.V.S. II Corps.	
		p.m.	Inspect Nos. 1, 2, 3 & 4 Coys. Div Train	
	2nd	am	Office routine.	
		p.m.	Routine	
	3rd	am	Visit & Inspect at 48th M.V.S.	
		p.m.	Inspect 36th Divl Supple undr 10 II Corps. Visited A.D.V.S.	
	4th	am	Office routine. Visit II Corps with DAQMG.	
		p.m.	Routine	
	5th	am	Routine	
		p.m.		
	6th	am	Visit I Corps. meet DDVS II Army.	
		p.m.	Vety Conference.	
	7th	am.	Visit Throat Specialist.	
		p.m.	Capt McClintock A.V.C. Cashiered by Sentence of General C.M.	
	8th	am. pm	Routine. Capt Guerlin A.V.C reports from leave.	
	9th	am pm	Routine.	

Army Form C. 2118.

D.A.D.V.S.,
36TH
(ULSTER) DIVISION.

WAR DIARY
or
INTELLIGENCE SUMMARY.
(Erase heading not required.)

Instructions regarding War Diaries and Intelligence Summaries are contained in F. S. Regs., Part II. and the Staff Manual respectively. Title pages will be prepared in manuscript.

Place	Date	Hour	Summary of Events and Information	Remarks and references to Appendices
Corbie	June 10	Am Pm	Routine	
Chalon	11th	Am. Pm	Routine	
	12th	Am.	Inspect at M.V.S. visit ADVS II Corps.	
		Pm	Routine	
	13th	Am	Inspect - Div Artly on Parade	
		Pm	Vety Conference. Inspect- S.A.A. 173 Coys A.S.C. M.V.S. D109 I.A. with Major Hunt - American Army Vet. eg team. Vety Administration etc to him.	
	14th	Am	Routine	
		Pm	Inspect - 153 Bde R.F.A.	
	15th	Am	Vet ADVS II Corps.	
		Pm	D Bty 9 173 Bde R.F.A. - Clerk sick	
	16th	Am Pm	Attend conference DADVS's at II Corps 10.30 to 12.30. Routine	
	17th	Am	Clerk still sick. Routine	
		Pm	DDVS Army & DDS Corps call & inspect M.V.S.	
	18th	Am Pm	Routine Inspect D 173 9 M.V.S.	
	19th	Am Pm	Routine	
	20th	Am Pm	Routine Veterinary Officers Conference.	

Army Form C. 2118.

WAR DIARY
or
INTELLIGENCE SUMMARY.
(Erase heading not required.)

Instructions regarding War Diaries and Intelligence Summaries are contained in F.S. Regs., Part II. and the Staff Manual respectively. Title pages will be prepared in manuscript.

DADVS 30th (DIVISION)

Place	Date	Hour	Summary of Events and Information	Remarks and references to Appendices
Corbehen Italian	21/6/18	Am	Routine. Inspect Rw Train at Rail Head with O.C 30 Res.	
		Pm		
	22	Am	Visit ADVS II Corps.	
		Pm	Routine	
	23	Am	Visit Corps	
		Pm	Visit ADVS II Corps	
	24	Am	Inspect 30 MG Bn & 107 Infy Bᵗⁿ with ADVS Corps	
		Pm	Inspect with ADV & DMS Rw Train PM Routine	
	25	Am	Inspect MYS. PM Visit II Army	
	26	Am	Conference DADVS's at II Corps. PM Routine	
	27	Am	Inspect Mashileuli Remounts PM Routine	
	28	Am	Visit ADVS Corps PM Routine	
	29	Am PM	Routine	
	30	Am PM	Routine Take over from ADVS II Corps who proceeds on leave 30ᵗʰ. Capt J.D Scott AVS taken over charge 1530/13 Bᵗⁿ RTA.	

A.S. Torner Major. DADVS 30 Div.

30/6/18.

WAR DIARY or INTELLIGENCE SUMMARY

Army Form C. 2118.

D.A.D.V.S. 36TH (ULSTER DIVISION)
No. VD 689
31.7.18

VD 34

19

Place	Date	Hour	Summary of Events and Information	Remarks and references to Appendices
COUTHOVE CHATEAU	July 1st	Am	Routine	
		Pm	Routine	
	2nd	Am	Proceed to II Corps to act as ADVS during absence of ADVS on 14 days leave	
			Visited Capt H Elwin OC 4th MVS to act for me during my absence. Orders to leave area. Stand own duties of ADVS II Corps. To Major Stewart DADVS 34 Div. comply with same	
		PM	Meer to Cassel. Office rept to Cassino MVS at H 34 D5. Sheet 27. Le Scheur	
Cassell	3rd	Am	Routine Returns etc.	
		Pm	Routine Pm Tety Conference	
	4th	Am	Routine	
	5th	Am	Rode round part of Area. See several units on leave bri Standsup	
		Pm	Visit & inspect the MVS at Le Scheur, also 173 B 3rd RFA	
	6th	Am	Rode round Area. Pm meet OC MVS & select site at P 34 D 1.2. for MVS near Officer's Mess	
			to No 72 Rue de Bergu Cassel	
	7th	Am	Routine visit - Laquelle to an ADVS of Corps that are moving to ZUYTPEENE	
		Pm	Routine	
	8th	Am, Pm	Routine	
	9th	Am	Attend Conference with ADVS X Corps	
TERDE GHEM		Pm	Inspect No 2 BMOV Coy Rec Train & MVS	

Army Form C. 2118.

WAR DIARY
or
INTELLIGENCE SUMMARY.
(Erase heading not required.)

D.A.D.V.S.
36TH
(ULSTER DIVISION)
No. V/9/689
Date 31·7·18

Instructions regarding War Diaries and Intelligence Summaries are contained in F. S. Regs., Part II. and the Staff Manual respectively. Title pages will be prepared in manuscript.

Place	Date	Hour	Summary of Events and Information	Remarks and references to Appendices
TERDEGHEM.	July 11th	am.	Ride round part of Area. Insped. No 1 Coy Train. & 109th Field Ambulance.	
		Pm	Routine	
	12th	am.	Vety Inspection. Visit round part of Area.	
		Pm	Routine reports returns.	
	13th	am, pm	Routine	
		am pm	Meet Capt Scott A.V.C. Insped. 153 & 173 Bde R.F.A. with him Routine	
For 14 and 15	14th	am pm	Meet Capt Miller A.V.C. & Insped. 107, 108 & 109 Infy Bdes. 16 R.I.R "P" 110 & 109	
			Field Ambulances. 36th Div M.G. Batln. 121, 122 & 150 R.E. Routine	
For 15 and 14	15th	am pm	Routine	
	16th	am pm	Insped. 36th D.A.C. Routine	
	17th	am pm	Insped. Div H Qrs. DH& R.A.M.R.E. 36 Div Signal Coy. & Div Train Routine	
	18th	am	Routine	
		pm	Vety Conference.	
	19th	am	Insped. with & O.C. Div 900 A.M.C. 109 Infy Bde 121, 122 Coys R.E.	
		pm	Routine	
	20th	am	Proced on 8 days leave to Paris. Hands over duties of DADVS to Capt Chown. O.C. 48 M.V.S.	
	21st	am pm.	Routine	
	22nd	am.	Attend Conference ADVS. X Corps.	
		pm.	Routine	

Army Form C. 2118.

D.A.D.V.S.,
36TH
(ULSTER) DIVISION
No W.D. 16 89
31.7.18

WAR DIARY
or
INTELLIGENCE SUMMARY.
(Erase heading not required.)

Instructions regarding War Diaries and Intelligence Summaries are contained in F. S. Regs., Part II and the Staff Manual respectively. Title pages will be prepared in manuscript.

Place	Date	Hour	Summary of Events and Information	Remarks and references to Appendices
TERDIGHEM	23/7/18	am & pm	Routine	
	24/7/18	am	ADVS & "CORPS visit & inspect MVS.	
		pm	Routine	
	25/7/18	am	Routine.	
		pm	Conference of VOs	
	26/7/18	am & pm	Routine	
	27/7/18	am	Routine	
		pm	Issue over & distribute 20 Remounts.	
	28/7/18	am	Routine	
		pm	Routine	
	29/7/18	am & pm	Routine	
	30/7/18	am & pm	Routine.	
	31/7/18	am & pm	Routine. Major Horne returns from Paris leave. Takes over duties of DADVS 36 Div from	
	1/8/18	am	Capt Chown OC 48 MVS	

A.J. Horne Major
DADVS 36 Division
31.7.18

WAR DIARY
or
INTELLIGENCE SUMMARY.
(Erase heading not required.)

Army Form C. 2118.

D.A.D.V.S.
36TH
(ULSTER) DIVISION
No. .... Date ....

Vol 35

Place	Date	Hour	Summary of Events and Information	Remarks and references to Appendices
TERDEGHEM	August 1st	AM	Insped with ADVS X Corps 153 Bde RFA	
		PM	Veterinary Officers Conference. Routine.	
	2nd	Am Pm	Very wet day. Reports & returns. Routine.	
	3rd	Am Pm	Routine. Insped 48 M.V.S.	
	4th	Am Pm	Church Parade 48 M.V.S. representative. Routine.	
	5th	Am Pm	Routine visit M.V.S. Base Units at refilling points. Insped 108 F.A. Condition V.G.	
	6th	Am Pm	Insped with ADVS X Corps 173 Bde R.F.A. Condition of all except "D" Very good "D" Poor. Steps being taken to try improve same.	
	7th	Am Pm	Routine visit 109 Fied Ambulance.	
	8th	Am Pm	Insped "D" 173 with CRA & Div enemy to end week. 6 teams from the Batteries of the Bde	
	9th	Am Pm	Vety Conference Capt. mule depots for Horse Lines	
	10th	Am Pm	Conference with ADVS X Corps go to Calais took round Vety Hospitals	
	11th	Am Pm	Routine	
	12th	Am Pm	Special Service at which King George's wagerail inspected at M.V.S.	
		Pm	Routine	
	13	Am	Insped M.V.S. 16 R.I.R. "P" Tpo 2 Dy Corps Bn Train Pm Routine.	

WAR DIARY
or
INTELLIGENCE SUMMARY.
(Erase heading not required.)

Army Form C. 2118.

D.A.D.V.S.
36TH
(ULSTER DIVISION)

Place	Date	Hour	Summary of Events and Information	Remarks and references to Appendices
TERDEGHEM	Aug 14	Am Pm	Routine	
	15	Am	Inspected 109 T.A.T. 1st R.I.R. "P" Pm Vety Conference. Routine	
	16	Am	A.D.V.S. E Corps Called. Routine Pm Yrd Wagon Lines Inspected with A.D.B.H.Q. 408 & 410 A.T.A	
	17	Am	D 153 Q 113 B 153 A 153 C 153 SAA & M.V.S. Routine Inspected with A.D.V.S.M.G. 121 & 122 R.E. Pm Routine	
	18	Am	Inspected 1st & 2nd T/15 R.I.R. 2nd about 4 horses on Light-Sr. Inspected D 173 all animals improving Pm Routine	
	19th	Am Pm	Inspected at M.V.S. Inspected 8 Dahihirli. 29 Remounts. Inspected 36th Signals. 7.0.1.6.4.0.2 Coy A.S.C.	
	20	Am Pm	Inspected A 96 173. 1st R.I.R. 1st R.I.Th.	
	21	Am Pm	Allied Committee on Selection of Troot Horses. Routine	
	22	Am Pm	Inspected at M.V.S. Conference S.V.O's.	
	23	Am Pm	Inspected 50 Remounts for Div Cav No.192 Sect D.A.C. Routine	
	24	Am Pm	Inspected 110 T.A.D. 1st R.I.R. Vety Conference	
	25	Am Pm	Routine	
	26	Am Pm	Inspected D.H.Q. + D 113 R.F.A. Routine	
	27	Am Pm	Inspected M.V.S. Routine	
	28	Am Pm	Routine 29th Inspected 10/173 15 R.I.R. 2 9 R.I.R. Vety Conference. 30= Am Pm Routine 31st August Am Pm Routine	

A. & Stoum Major D.A.D.V.S. 36 Div
31.8.18

Army Form C. 2118.

Original

D.A.D.V.S.
36TH
(ULSTER DIVISION)
No. VS/45F
1.10.18

WAR DIARY
or
INTELLIGENCE SUMMARY.
(Erase heading not required.)

Instructions regarding War Diaries and Intelligence Summaries are contained in F. S. Regs., Part II. and the Staff Manual respectively. Title pages will be prepared in manuscript.

Place	Date	Hour	Summary of Events and Information	Remarks and references to Appendices
St Sylvestre Capelle	1-9-18	am	Capt Chown departs on 10 days leave pending transfer to Egyptian Army. DADVS taken charge of MFS. & Vety charge of Capt Chown's units. Visit- Stables over M.V.S.	
		Pm	Inspect new VS Area at Becker	
Becker	2nd	am	Move to Becker. Select site for M.V.S. at R28 D.8.9. Inspect 121, 122 & 150 R.E. Estoblishmts	
		Pm	Advance Vety AS Post at R35 A.3.0 Sheet 27.	
Mont des Cats	3rd	am	Visit X Corps & arrange to ADVS arrangements made.	
		Pm	Move Office from Becker to Mont des Cats. Visit HQ Train Nº7 Coy A.S.C. & Signals	
	4th	am	Visit M.VS. & withdraw AS Post.	
		Pm	Visit & inspect 36 Sep. No2 Coy Train & Div HQ.	
	5th	am	Visit M.V.S. & 36 Signals	
		Pm	Vety Conference	
St Jeans Capelle	6th	am	Move Office HQ to St Jeans Capelle. Reconnoitre around Croy de Poperinghe Westoft Farm meur	
			Eylere & Ravelsberg for Water for Wagon Lines. P.M. Work at M.V.S.	
	7th	am	Inspect 107 & 108 Infy B'de. Nos. 16 R.I.R "B" 121 & 122 R.E. P.M. Pay men at M.V.S. Evacuate 14 horses. Office etc.	

Army Form C. 2118.

D.A.D.V.S.,
36TH
(ULSTER DIVISION).
No. 7/7958
1.10.18

WAR DIARY
or
INTELLIGENCE SUMMARY.
(Erase heading not required.)

Instructions regarding War Diaries and Intelligence Summaries are contained in F. S. Regs., Part II. and the Staff Manual respectively. Title pages will be prepared in manuscript.

Place	Date	Hour	Summary of Events and Information	Remarks and references to Appendices
St Jean Capell	Sept 8	A.M.	Visit No 2 Sect DAC when 57 animals were killed & 20 wounded by Bombs. Enemy. Visit MVS. Visit D/153. When the whole Battery was affected with some obscure disease probably gas poisoning. 16 were all of very ill one dead. Arrang for ADVS X Corps to come over after lunch. Visit D/153 with ADVS X Corps. Visit M.V.S.	
	9th	A.M.	Visit D/153 with DDVS II Army ADVS X Corps Gas Officer DVO. P.M. Inspect 90 Remounts	
	10.	A.M.	Visit M.V.S. Richeboule 45 Remounts. Visit D/153. Routine	
	11.	am pm.	Routine.	
	12.	am pm.	Visit MVS D/139/153. MVS Routine.	
	13.	am pm.	Visit 30 Squads. Inspect with V.O. I/C 109 Bt. 150 R.E. MG Bn. 15th Bn M.P. Search for Clapping place with DAAG. Visit MVS Pay our staff men.	
	14	am	Inspect with ADVS X Corps D/173 Condition greatly improved. P.M Routine	
	15	am pm	Routine.	
	16	am	Visit D/173 A/173 D/153. Inspect their Visit 380 works at MVS. PM Routine	
	17	am pm	Inspect D/173 & 153. Casualty wounded 12 from D/153 convalescent after poisoning RO MVS work Visit ADVS X Corps.	
	18	am	Rode round area with ADD & q. Orders to move visit X Corps new area during the evening	

2353 Wt. W2544/1454 700,000 5/15 D. D. & L. A.D.S.S./Forms/C. 2118.

WAR DIARY or INTELLIGENCE SUMMARY

Army Form C. 2118.

D.A.D.V.S. 36TH (ULSTER DIVISION) No VD 1958 1.10.18

Place	Date	Hour	Summary of Events and Information	Remarks and references to Appendices
	Sept			
St Jeans Capell	19	AM	Routine interview Capt Miller visit division M.V.S. Report to ADVS II Corps. PM Routine	
	20	AM	Go round new Arc. Malan Houthulp Monchurst & Esquelber with CADVMy vet M.V.S	
		PM	at Esquelber. Move to St Jeans der Biezen	
St Jeans dr Biezen	21	AM	Vet M.V.S. PM Capt Stiven reports to take over duties of M.V.S. Take him to Esquelbec. PM out - run Trolley hand over.	
	22	AM PM	Vet M.V.S. & See Capt Miller. Routine	
	23	AM	Routine. PM Routine Reclam horse of 14 Div Train midnight	
	24	AM	Inspect animals at Reception Camp. SAA Sct. 16 RIR P. 15D01.21 R 2.	
		PM	Inspect Div HQ M.M.P. 36 Squads.	
	25	AM PM	Routine.	
	26	PM	Take over 5 Cav Bde AHT. vet MVS at Esquelbec & They Bri. N°2 Coy ASC.	
	27	AM	Reconnoitre Vlamintinghe for MVS site. PM move to VOGELTJE convent.	
VOGELTJE	28	AM	Routine. PM Routine MVS moves to H2 B 5.5 Sheet 28. Vet ADVS II Corps.	
"	29	AM	Vet advance OHQ at Ramparts Ypres. Move MVS to 29 H6 B9.0 Vet ADVS II Corps. with him to 29 MVS	
YPRES	30	AM	Vet 109 Bde MVS Div Tran & SAA move to Ramparts Ypres. Vet advance OHQ at 28/K7025 Biecelaere Other Routine.	DADVS 36 Div

A.S Nouen Major DADVS 36 Div
1.10.18

WAR DIARY
or
INTELLIGENCE SUMMARY.
(Erase heading not required.)

Army Form C. 2118.

D.A.D.V.S.
36TH
(ULSTER DIVISION)
No V.D.2079
Date 13.11.18.

Vol 38

Place	Date	Hour	Summary of Events and Information	Remarks and references to Appendices
YPRES Ramparts	October 1st		Routine not round front areas with AAQMG re much Mtc Transport on roads. reconnoitre different roads to prevent absence Transport Lines	
Junction Camp St Jean	2		Moved from Ypres to St Jean Junction Camp. Visit MVS established A.V.P at J12 D2.8 BECELAERE interview Capt Scott	
	3		Visit A.V.P. re Transport of 107. 108 Bde 109 Bde. 16 R.I.R.P. 153 Bde 3rd R.T.A. Vety Conference. Visit ADVS II Corps.	
	4th		Visit TERHAND. Call at A.V.P. Lieut Chalmers reports for duty vice Capt Guerlain A.V.C.	
	5th		Visit MVS & DAC Divisional 40 Remounts 30 to R.A. & 10 to Signal Routine.	
	6th		Visit A.V.P & all Brigades with AAQMG, Visit ADVS II Corps. inspect at MVS en route Routine	
	7th			
	8th		Go to advance Remount Section at Zulpine in charge of Q.O.C. & A.D.C. then on to 5 Remount Depot Calais where Select 2 chargers for G.O.C. Stay night in Calais	
	9th		Return from Calais 2.30 p.m. as til 60 Remounts for 36 in before leaving Routine	
	10th		Visit MVS meet ADVS II Corps then Veterinary Conference Routine	
	11th		Inspect 173 Brigade RTA all in satisfactory condition. Call at Corps ree ADVS Routine	
	12th		Conference at II Corps Visit No 2 V.B.S. Inspect at MVS. See Capt Muller AVC Routine	

WAR DIARY
or
INTELLIGENCE SUMMARY.
(Erase heading not required.)

Army Form C. 2118.

Place	Date	Hour	Summary of Events and Information	Remarks and references to Appendices
	Oct.			
Junction Camp St Jean	13		9/0 to Proven b/m Inspr. Takes over Remounts. Distributed to Remounts at MVS. Routine.	
	14		Visit all Transport Lines. AVP. & MVS. All animals in satisfactory condition. MVS moved to D 30 Central.	
Beculaere	15		Move from St Jean to Beculaere. Open at 12 noon. MVS moves from 28/J12 D2.8 to K17 A 2.6 approximate. Meet ADVS II Corps. Inspect at MVS & RwTrain Office. Routine.	
"	16		Office visit 107 Bst DAC. RwTrain & MVS on to advance HQ at L15 C 9.0/28. See HQ horses. MVS moves to K17. A2.6. No advance post out.	
LEDE GHEM	17		Move to Ledeghem. 28/J26 D 90. MVS moves to 26/L1 C 9 0. See much RwTransport en route. Office Routine. Vety Conference.	
"	18		Visit forward area & advance DHQ with AADVS. See much Transport. 2 B 3rd RA. 107 & 109 Sufs horses. DAC. 16 R.I.R.P. 1508/121 Q 8. Reports & returns.	
LENDEL EDE	19		Move Office to Beer to LENDELEDE Shut 29. A 18 C entral. Inspect at MVS 9/0/82 DAC.	
	20		Inspect 36 MG Bn with Capt Miller. Move MVS to A22 B 8.8/29. Routine	
	21		Inspect 31 Squad. with Capt Steven. See Capt Scott & Capt Miller. Visit 128 RIR Transport. Routine.	
	22		Inspect Squads M G Coy "B". HQ 36 Div 7th P with ADVS II Corps. Visit Corps HQ & MVS. Routine.	

Army Form C. 2118.

WAR DIARY
or
INTELLIGENCE SUMMARY.
(Erase heading not required.)

Instructions regarding War Diaries and Intelligence Summaries are contained in F.S. Regs., Part II. and the Staff Manual respectively. Title pages will be prepared in manuscript.

D.A.D.V.S. 36TH (ULSTER) DIVISION
No. VO 2079
Date 1.11.18

Place	Date	Hour	Summary of Events and Information	Remarks and references to Appendices
LENDE LEDE	23.		Visit M.V.S. 2nd pet 150 R.I.R. Routine.	
"	24.		Vety conference. Routine.	
"	25.		Reports & returns. Routine.	
"	26.		Visit 9 moped at M.V.S. Visit 16 R.I.R. "P" & S.A.A. Section. See annuals M.V.S. moves to 29/B 21 D 5. 50 Remounts for other units & 159 for Div Arty Condition B Type good. See on Road.	
"	27.		O C 48 In V S calls & hands over to Lieut. gun on leave - Routine to take act remts - Routine	
"	28.		Move from Lendelede to Belleghem M V S motors to LAUWE on 29/18 arrange over Bn fell from 34 Div so with A A & Arty to I Corps 9 call on A.D.V.S.	
Belleghem	29.		Proceed on 14 days leave to England. Capt. Stevens O C 48 In V S taken over duties of acting D A D V S.	
"	30.		Routine. Arranges for horses from units the sent to M.Y.S. for clipping etc.	
"	31.		Conference. A.D.V.S. + Capts visits M.V.S. Routine for clipping to patterns.	J.H. Stevens Capt.
				b A.D.V.S 36 Div

WAR DIARY
or
INTELLIGENCE SUMMARY.
(Erase heading not required.)

Army Form C. 2118.

November 1918

36TH (ULSTER) DIVISION

Place	Date	Hour	Summary of Events and Information	Remarks and references to Appendices
M Bsllegkun Maulian	Nov 1		Routine	
	2		Routine	
	3		Routine	
	4		Routine	
	5		Moved H.Q.	
	6		Routine. ADVS visited 173 Bde R.F.A.	
	7		Routine. Conference.	
	8		Routine. Reports re horses 153 Bde R.F.A.	
	9		Routine. ADVS visited 153 Bde R.F.A.	
	10		Routine. Remounts arrived MVS	
	11		Routine. Distributed remounts from MVS	mules & horses from Divers Mtcals, mules &c
	12		Routine. Major ADVS XV Corps.	
	13		Routine. Conference	
	14		Routine	
	15		Routine	
Mouscron	16		Routine	
	17		Routine	
	18		Routine	
	19		Routine	
	20		Inspect at MVS. Conference at Corps. Major A L Horn reported for duty from leave	
	21		Routine. Vety Conference. Sent 28 horses for transfer to 9th Division. Officer etc	
	22		Inspect 173 Bde R.F.A.	
	23		" 153 Bde R.F.A.	
	24		Routine	
	25		Inspect 36 DAC. meet ADVS II Corps. Routine	

Army Form C. 2118.

WAR DIARY
or
INTELLIGENCE SUMMARY.
(Erase heading not required.)

November 1918

Place	Date	Hour	Summary of Events and Information	Remarks and references to Appendices
Moascar	26		Inspect 1st R.I.R. 108 Field Ambulance 109 T.M. 110 T.M. 12th R.I.R. 1st R Innis Fus 121 R.E. 108 H.Q. 122 R.E. 2 R.I.R. 16 R.I.R.(P) 15th R.I.R. All very satisfactory	
	27		Inspect 9th R Innis Fus. 150 R.E. 1st R Innis Fus. 2nd R Innis Fus. 109 H.Q. all satisfactory	
	28		Inspect 36 M.G. Btn. all satisfactory. Routine Veterinary Officers Conference.	
	29		Inspect 36 Div Squadron + Div H.Q. Select cut in Moascar for M.V.S. Routine	
	30		Routine. Inspect. 9 R.I. Fus satisfactory	

A.S. Glover M.R.C.V.S
D.A.D.V.S 36.11.18
NADVS 30.11.18

Army Form C. 2118.

D.A.D.V.S.
36TH
(ULSTER) DIVISION
No 2D.23.27
to 1/1/19

WAR DIARY
or
INTELLIGENCE SUMMARY.
(Erase heading not required.)

Instructions regarding War Diaries and Intelligence Summaries are contained in F. S. Regs., Part II. and the Staff Manual respectively. Title pages will be prepared in manuscript.

Place	Date	Hour	Summary of Events and Information	Remarks and references to Appendices
MOUSE RON	December 1st		Inspected 36th Divisional Train Routine	
	2nd		Routine 48 MVS moved to Mourcron.	
	3rd		Routine go to XY Corps to see ADVS.	
	4th		Proceed to Rouen with CAB & HQ Capt Stirven carries on duties of DADVS	
	5th			
	6th		Return from Rouen for duty	
	7th		Routine	
	8th		Inspected Div Riding School Routine	
	9th		Routine took over duties of OC 48 MVS when Capt Stirven proceeds on 10 days Paris leave	
	10th		Inspected MVS. See Arch Brown Sigs PAT Coy met VO/c Mi Arty Routine	
	11th		Inspected MVS	
	12th		All gay on MVS various transcend, attend a Presdtn Proc'd on Stevenson Smith Vet Conyeur	
	13th		Presd man Committi	
	14th		Visit MVS & THQ Brown Call on DDVS V Army	
	15th		Visit MVS se Div Arty on roads. met VO/c DAC.	
	16th			

Army Form C. 2118.

D.A.D.V.S.
36TH
(ULSTER) DIVISION.

WAR DIARY
or
INTELLIGENCE SUMMARY.
(Erase heading not required.)

Instructions regarding War Diaries and Intelligence Summaries are contained in F.S. Regs., Part II. and the Staff Manual respectively. Title pages will be prepared in manuscript.

Place	Date	Hour	Summary of Events and Information	Remarks and references to Appendices
MOUSCRON	17		Inspect. A153. Vis. V.A.C.	
	18		Inspect. Wat. M.V.S. Routine	
	19		Prov. Man Committee. Vety Conference.	
	20		Inspect. A113. C&D 153. Vis. M.V.S. Routine	
	21		Routine	
	22		Routine. Vis. ADVS XV Corps.	
	23		Routine	
	24		Call on ADVS XV Corps. Routine	
	25		Routine. Vis. M.V.S.	
	26		Routine. Vis. M.V.S. Veterinary Conference.	
	27		ADVS XV Corps Called. Book for Concentration Horse Camp amongst numerous	
			Vist & Inspect. 48 M.V.S. Routine Reports & Returns	
	28		Conference of DADVS's at ADVS's XV Corps re Demobilization of Horses. Routine	
	29		Routine	
	30		Routine. Veterinary Conference on "Demobilization of Horses" at V.O's present.	
	31		Examine all Horses of A113 for Demobilization Clearance declaration.	

A S Moores Major
DADVS 36th Ulster Division
Jan 1st 1919.

21
36/

Army Form C. 2118.

D.A.D.V.S.
36TH
(ULSTER) DIVISION.
No V8 2473
Date 13.2.19

No V8 2471

WAR DIARY
or
INTELLIGENCE SUMMARY.
(Erase heading not required.)

Instructions regarding War Diaries and Intelligence Summaries are contained in F. S. Regs., Part II. and the Staff Manual respectively. Title pages will be prepared in manuscript.

Place	Date	Hour	Summary of Events and Information	Remarks and references to Appendices
MOUSCRON	Jan 1st		Examine & Classify all horses of B 173 R.F.A.	
	2nd		" " " " C 173 "	Vety Conference
	3rd		" " " " D 173 "	
	4th		" " " " A 153 "	
	5		" " " " No 3 Coy 36 Div Train	
	6		Sit as President of Board to examine men as S.S. Roulries	
	7		Classify all horses of B 153 R.F.A. & H.Q. 153. Roulries	
	8		" " " " C 153 " & H.Q. 173 Roulries	
	9		" " " " D 153 " Vety Conference Roulries	
	10		" " " " No 1 Section D.A.C.	
	11		" " " " No 2 " "	
	12		" " " " No 1, 2 & 4 Coys R.A.S.C.	
	13		" " " " No 3 Sect. D.A.C. & D.A.C. H.Q.	
	14		" " " " 107 Infy Bde H.Q.	
	15		" " " " 108 " "	

(A8011) Wt. W17721/M2031 750,000 5/17 **Sch. 52** Forms/C2118/14 D. D. & L., London, E.C.

Army Form C. 2118.

WAR DIARY
or
INTELLIGENCE SUMMARY.
(Erase heading not required.)

D.A.D.V.S.,
36TH
(ULSTER) DIVISION.
No WD 2473
Date 1.2.19

Place	Date	Hour	Summary of Events and Information	Remarks and references to Appendices
MOUSCRON	Jan 16		Classify & Examine all animals 109 Infy Bryde. D.H.Q. Veterinary Conference	
	17		Classify & Examine all animals 150 R.E. 108 T.A.	
	18		" " " " 121 & 122 R.E. & 109 T.A.	
	19		Visit R.A.H.Q. See cases of 153 Bde R.T.A.	
	20		Classify & Examine all animals A&D Coys T.H.Q. 36 M.G. Bn. Visit XV Corps D.D.V.S. a.D.V.S.	
	21		" " " " B&C Coys M.G. Bn. 110 T.A. D. 16 R.I.R. "P" Routine	
	22		" " " " 36 Signals, M.Y.S. D.H.Q. T.M.B. Completed	
	23		Classification of all animals of the 36th Division	
	24		Visit A173 to inspect malleined horses. Veterinary Conference.	
	25		Routine	
	26		Inspect at M.Y.S. Visit 1st R.I.R. re classify on HD. home from D to B. Routine.	
	27		Inspect at M.Y.S. Examine & classify remaining few horses of Div. not seen before	
	28		Examine all of Div. Train.	
	29		Routine	
	30		Allied Conference at XV Corps. Conference gyro's at Div. H.Q.	
	31		On Rising School Board. Routine	

A.S. Tomer Major
D.A.D.V.S. 36 Ulster Division
31.1.19.

WAR DIARY or INTELLIGENCE SUMMARY.

Army Form C. 2118.

D.A.D.V.S.
36TH (ULSTER) DIVISION
No. V/2583
Date 1.2.19

Vol 4 2

Place	Date 1919	Hour	Summary of Events and Information	Remarks and references to Appendices
MOUSCRON	Feby 1st		Inspect at M.V.S. Visit A.D.Q. Office. Inspect H.Q. Horses. Routine	
	2		Routine, examine Capt. Scott R.T.A. in Horsemanship	
	3		Routine	
	4		Visit M.V.S. see Horses etc. Routine	
	5		Inspect at M.V.S. visit A.D.Q.	
	6		Visit A.D.Q. M.V.S & R.R. Veterinary Conference. Visit sick get horses hidden at M.V.S.	
	7		Routine	
	8		Office. Routine	
	9		Routine	
	10		Take over duties of A.D.V.S XV Corps in addition to ordinary duties. Inspect 153, 13th RTA see horses. Confer with A.D.V.S XV Corps. Routine.	
	11		Visit M.V.S inspect Very Office. Take over duties of A.D.V.S XV Corps. Horse & aux Rules of A.D.V.S XV Corps.	
	12		Inspect at M.V.S. Routine	
	13		Routine Very Conference.	
	14		Routine Visit M.V.S & Squadron Report. Routine	
	15		Visit 173 Bde R.T.A D.A.C see V.O.s Visit M.V.S evacuate of Animals Routine	
	16		Visit M.V.S Routine	
	17		Receive orders to be prepared to hand over Officers to England en route to India. Routine	
	18		Visit 36 m.g. Bn. see Team Horses. Visit M.V.S. evacuate of Horses of Divisn Routine	

WAR DIARY or INTELLIGENCE SUMMARY

Army Form C. 2118.

D.A.D.V.S. 36TH (ULSTER) DIVISION.

Place	Date	Hour	Summary of Events and Information	Remarks and references to Appendices
Mouvron	Feby 19		Visit M.V.S. evacuate 3 horses not using. Visit Major Lind. Routine	
	20		Visit M.V.S. not over to ADVS Corps. Vety Conference. Routine	
	21		Inspect at 178 F.A. Mob. M.V.S. Reports Returns. Routine.	
	22		Visit M.V.S. took their evacuated 2 horses. Inspect 100 animals dismounted 9 Routine.	
	23		Visit M.V.S. Routine. Capt Thomas R.A.V.C. reports passing orders presumed to be a taking over	
	24		Hand over to Capt W H Thomas. Have VO's to meet him. Visit M.V.S evacuate 3 horses. Routine.	
	25		Hand over to Capt W H Thomas. Routine	
	26		Leave 36th Welsh Division having handed over duties of DADVS 36 Welsh Division to Capt (acting Major) W H Thomas R.A.V.C. Proceed to Boulogne for embarkation preparing 25 War Office on arrival.	

A.S. Thom Major DADVS 36th Welsh Division.

70m. 26/2/19.

| | 26 | | Assumed duties of D.A.D.V.S. 36th Welsh Dn. Reported to Dn & A.D.V.S. XV Corps that duties of D.A.D.V.S. had been taken over by me. | |

WAR DIARY
or
INTELLIGENCE SUMMARY.

(Erase heading not required.)

Army Form C. 2118.

D.A.D.V.S. 36TH (ULSTER DIVISION)

Place	Date	Hour	Summary of Events and Information	Remarks and references to Appendices
Moascar	Feb. 27. 28		Visit. M.V.S. Conference with V.O.S. Representatives. Inspect 153 Brigade R.F.A. Representatives. Rankin. Watchman. Major R.A.V.C. D.A.D.V.S. 36 Ulster 28.2.19.	

Army Form C. 2118.

D.A.D.V.S.,
36TH
(ULSTER) DIVISION.
No V.S. 2655
Date 25/3/14

WAR DIARY
or
INTELLIGENCE SUMMARY.
(Erase heading not required.)

Instructions regarding War Diaries and Intelligence Summaries are contained in F. S. Regs., Part II. and the Staff Manual respectively. Title pages will be prepared in manuscript.

Place	Date	Hour	Summary of Events and Information	Remarks and references to Appendices
Lucknow	March 1.		Inspect animals 173 Brig: RFA. Report returns. Routine.	V.S. 39 erased
"	2.		Routine	
"	3.		Inspected all animals 34th F.A.C. N.C.O. bury animals 153 Brig. RFA.	
"	4.		Visit M.V.S. Routine. Reports returns.	
"	5.		Inspected animals 107 +108 Infy Brigades.	
	6.		Conferences with all V.O.S. Inspected animals 122 Coy R.E. Reports returns.	
	7.		Visit M.V.S. Reports returns. Inspected animals 109 Infy Brig.	
	8.		Conferred with A.D.V.S. XV Corps. Routine. Reports returns.	
	9.		Visit M.V.S.	
	10.		Inspect animals 16th R. I. Rifles & Nos 107, 109, 110 Field Ambulances.	
	11.		Arranged with V.O. to RA unit for mallein test of mx horses R.A. unit. Inspected 100 x animals mallein for stoppage to Anwells Collecting Comp. Routine.	
	17.			
	12.		Visit 15. V.E.C. W. Comps with OC as to Forradically sale of horses at Hence. Reports returns.	
	13.		Conducted sale of 99 horses and 3 mules at Hence	
	14.		Conference with all V.O.S. Reports returns. Routine	
	15.		Visit M.V.S. Reports returns. Routine	

Army Form C. 2118.

WAR DIARY
or
INTELLIGENCE SUMMARY.
(Erase heading not required.)

Instructions regarding War Diaries and Intelligence Summaries are contained in F. S. Regs., Part II. and the Staff Manual respectively. Title pages will be prepared in manuscript.

Place	Date	Hour	Summary of Events and Information	Remarks and references to Appendices
Lucknow	March 16		Routine. Arranged for mallein testing of all remaining X horses in Bde.	
	17		Routine.	
	18		Reprobationers. Conferred with V.O.S. re R.A. units no trouble taking Jamnails under their own charge. Routine.	
	19		Visit M.V.S. Reprobationers.	
	20		Conference with all V.O.S. Inspected 6 HQ. XT Corps troops unit a.T.V.T.	
	21		Visit M.V.S. Reprobationers. Routine.	
	22		L. Corr Corps, bringing into its "Equipment" in charge, R.A. unit. Routine.	
	23		Reprobationers. Routine. Visit M.V.S.	
	24		Officer of A.D.V.T. 36th (Ulster) Dr. ceased at 12:00 hrs today in accordance with instructions contained in 3658 W.W. 250/D/57 A (d) 21.3.10.	

W.J.Thomas
Major R.A.V.C.
D.A.D.V.T. 36 (Ulster) Div

www.ingramcontent.com/pod-product-compliance
Lightning Source LLC
Chambersburg PA
CBHW082009220426
43670CB00014B/2587